Ubiquitous Photography

Digital Media and Society

Ubiquitous Photography

MARTIN HAND

polity

First published in 2012 by Polity Press

Polity Press
65 Bridge Street
Cambridge CB2 1UR, UK

Polity Press
350 Main Street
Malden, MA 02148, USA

ISBN-13: 978-0-7456-4714-2
ISBN-13: 978-0-7456-4715-9 (pb)

A catalogue record for this book is available from the British Library.

Typeset in 10.25 on 13 pt Scala
by Servis Filmsetting Ltd, Stockport, Cheshire
Printed and bound in Great Britain by MPG Books Group, Bodmin, Cornwall.

The publisher has used its best endeavours to ensure that the URLs for external websites referred to in this book are correct and active at the time of going to press. However, the publisher has no responsibility for the websites and can make no guarantee that a site will remain live or that the content is or will remain appropriate.

Every effort has been made to trace all copyright holders, but if any have been inadvertently overlooked the publisher will be pleased to include any necessary credits in any subsequent reprint or edition.

For further information on Polity, visit our website: www.politybooks.com

Contents

Detailed Contents

List of Figures

Acknowledgements

I am grateful for the financial support of the Social Sciences and Humanities Research Council (Canada) in supporting this research during 2006–2010. Particular thanks go to research assistants Ashley Scarlett, Sonja Solomun, Kelly Reid, Jennifer Harrington, Kimberley DeWolff and Jessica Grimaldi. I offer thanks to all participants and experts I have encountered in Library and Archives Canada, National Gallery of Canada, George Eastman House, whose help went way beyond what I might have expected. Sincere thanks to all those anonymous interviewees for sparing their time in explaining their diverse engagements with film and digital photography, the substance of which forms the rationale for this book.

I still owe a favour to Brian Woods, Paul Rosen, David Skinner and Andrew Webster for enabling me to get into this area. I am very grateful for the insights of Barry Sandywell, Elizabeth Shove, Joan Schwartz, Sergio Sismondo, Leah MacFadyen, Danielle Robichaud, Tara Milbrandt, Susan Salhany and graduate students in SOCY931. I would like to thank Victoria Millious and two anonymous readers for their helpful suggestions.

Some elements of the chapters have been presented in different forms at the Kingston Photographic Society, Kingston, Ontario, 2007; the McGill University Department of Art History and Communications Speaker Series, Montreal, 2008; the Canadian Sociology and Anthropology Association Annual Conference, University of British Columbia, 2008; the Feeling Photography Conference, the Toronto Photography Seminar and the Centre for the Study of the

United States, University of Toronto, 2008; the Society for Social Studies of Science Annual Meeting, Washington, DC, 2009; the Technoscience Salon, University of Toronto, 2010; and the British Sociological Association Annual Conference, London School of Economics, 2011.

Many thanks to the enormous patience, skill and encouragement of Andrea Drugan and colleagues at Polity in allowing me to take somewhat longer than anyone anticipated.

Unreserved thanks as always to my wonderful family, whose generosity is immeasurable.

The publishers gratefully acknowledge the following for permission to reproduce copyright material:
Page 10, © Jen Grantham/ iStockphoto.com; 13, © Ron Haviv/VII/Corbis; 71, © Laurel Friedman; 90, Creative Commons Kalleboo; 108, Creative Commons Tom Photos; 110, Creative Commons Jaqian; 118, Creative Commons Yellow Shark; 169, 179, © Andrea Drugan.

CHAPTER ONE

Ubiquitous Photography: A Short Introduction

Over the last two decades digital images have become ubiquitous aspects of daily life in advanced capitalist societies. The rise of digital photography as an ordinary practice has transformed the landscape of visual communication and culture: events, activities, moments, objects and people are 'captured' and distributed as images on an unprecedented scale. Alongside dramatic changes in the relative dominance of the photographic, computer and telecommunications industries and the use of digital images in journalism, art, tourism, archives and medicine, people routinely make and store thousands of digital photos recording the eventful and the mundane. Many of these are distributed by email or through web applications such as Flickr and Facebook, producing searchable archives of everyday minutiae. Others remain in private collections, albums and traditional modes of display and viewing. Some become intellectual property or commodities, while others assume the potential to shape global events. It is hard to imagine any aspect of contemporary life that has not become visual content, as communications and social relations are increasingly mediated through or accompanied by digital images. The weaving of *photographies* – as images and ideas, as devices and techniques, and as practices – into every corner of contemporary society and culture produces quite a different scenario from that envisaged during the late twentieth century. Where many once imagined a future of digital simulation and virtual reality, we now arguably have the opposite: the visual publicization of ordinary life in a ubiquitous photoscape.

This book examines the current pervasiveness of still photography and imaging in relation to academic debates about digital culture. The simple observation framing it is that we are witnessing the death of film but the proliferation of photographies. This is true in terms of the disappearance of film manufacturing and processing, the production of film cameras, the availability of darkrooms, and the use of film in anything other than specialist domains or niche communities of practice. Since 1999, there has been a decline in the number of film-based photographs and a dramatic growth in the creation of images using digital cameras. For example, in 2002 there were 27.5 million digital still cameras purchased worldwide, compared with 63 million analogue (film-based) cameras (Lyman and Varian 2003). Worldwide shipments of digital cameras increased to 119 million in 2008 and, at the time of writing, are projected to be 120 million in 2011, while film cameras have all but disappeared (*Digital Photography Review* 2011).

As photography is woven into digital media, it is becoming something of a banality in terms of its corporate, institutional and everyday prevalence. At the level of popular cultural practices, new social media have come to be increasingly visual, from websites that allow for free image hosting and sharing such as Photobucket and Flickr, indexing sites such as Digg, and social networking sites such as Facebook and MySpace, to the increased use of photos in blogs and personal web pages. In terms of the extent of viewable digital images, at the time of writing the 'online photo management and sharing' site Flickr hosts over 4 billion images, with almost 5,000 images being uploaded per minute. Similarly, the visual content storage and sharing site Photobucket currently receives 4.7 million images on a daily basis. It is perhaps surprising that Facebook hosts more photos than the explicitly photo-orientated Flickr, with over 15 billion in 2009 and current uploads of a staggering 4 billion per month. These vast dynamic repositories of images provide a glimpse into the massive production of photos in the conduct of everyday life. Similarly, the expansion of corporately managed visual content appears exponential. At GettyImages.com, users have access to 24.7 million images, with a variety of rights-controlled and royalty-free stock images available.

Taken as a whole, from the use of images in reporting, advertising and institutional practices of record keeping to the vast numbers of digital snapshots taken in daily life, contemporary Western cultures involve unprecedented levels of *visual mediation*. This is partly an outcome of the ever increasing ownership of digital cameras. But it also entails a vast increase in the use of wired and wireless networking technologies, of laptops, tablets and cellphones that now incorporate visual technologies and a variety of capturing, storing and distributing practices. Alongside the convergence of the camera and the computer, there is an emerging interplay between the digital camera and the phone, smartphone and cameraphones, particularly in the Asian economies, where over 80 per cent of cell/mobile phones are now also image-capture devices. According to market research forecasts, worldwide shipments of cameraphones will jump from over 700 million units in 2007 to surpass 1.3 billion in 2012 (Infotrends 2010). These devices in turn enable and are enabled by new visual rhetorics and techniques, all of which are producing a novel landscape of screens and images. In all the above senses, digital imaging has shifted from a professional or specialized process to a routine and unavoidable aspect of everyday life. At the same time, what was once amateur or snapshot photography has become potentially global in scope.

Personal photography is the focus of this book partly because of the clearly identifiable increase in image-making as an ordinary aspect of people's lives. A second reason is that, as Shove (2003) has convincingly argued, the domain of the ordinary is precisely what should concern sociologists and others when trying to understand social, cultural and technical change. Theories of digital imaging and photography have been skewed mostly towards philosophical concerns with the ontology of the image or with the professional domains of photojournalism and art photography. As a counterpoint to this, I suggest that the domain of personal photography provides a particularly useful way of identifying emergent aspects of sociotechnical stability and change in the domain of digital culture.

For these reasons, the confines of photography studies, with their primary focus on the visual image, are necessarily limited in their scope for understanding the broader dynamics of digitization. This is not a book about images primarily, and it is not written by a professional or serious photographer. It is a book about the dynamic constellation of practices under the umbrella of ubiquitous photography, and how such practices of making, storing, distributing and displaying images are emerging on the ground. However, I argue that such a scenario requires analyses that pay serious attention to the theory and history of photography but equally are able to move well beyond those boundaries. While this is partly a story of rapid technological change – the digitization of photography – it is also an investigation of how the more subtle and precise ways in which digitization relates to a variety of image-making practices and technological devices has become compelling territory for understanding the dynamics of digital media and society.

Personal and ubiquitous photographies

> Twenty-two years after the arrival of the first consumer digital camera, Western culture is now characterized by ubiquitous photography. (Rubenstein and Sluis 2008: 9)

The above observation suggests radical change at the present time, but this is not the first moment in history when photography has been considered 'ubiquitous'. As Hirsch (2000: 175) observes, the *New York Times* ran a story on 20 August 1884 concerning an 'epidemic' of cameras, with amateurs described as 'camera lunatics' training their cameras on those simply walking down the street. The scenario of having one's picture taken unawares seemed radically intrusive, even though there were relatively few hand-held cameras in circulation by today's standards. Nonetheless, familiar responses emerged: concerns about the acceptable boundaries between public and private, the suitability of previously unseen objects or actions, the breakdown of societal boundaries of decency and 'good taste', as places were 'besieged' with amateur photographers, and so on. In order to understand what may be different at the present time, it is worth briefly highlighting some of the ways in which personal photography has evolved, all of which will be explored in more detail throughout the book.

The evolution of personal photographies

To begin, we should ask what we mean by *personal* photography and how this relates to *ubiquitous* photography. Personal photography includes those photographic practices and images that are inextricably part of personal life – whether the individual taking of pictures, the images we use to represent ourselves, the pictures we collect or display for ourselves, or the sharing of pictures with others as part of personal communication. These forms may be distinguished from institutional, governmental, scientific and broadly professional forms of photography and imaging, although the categories have latterly become blurred, as will be explained. The story of personal photography involves its vast expansion and diversification over the last one hundred and fifty years, in tandem with technical, socioeconomic and cultural shifts in personal life. While personal photography has often been located within the domestic sphere or the family, it cannot be reduced to amateur, private, popular, family or snapshot photography as if all these were the same. Personal photography is inextricably tied to broader changes in what counts as 'family', how social identities have shifted in relation to patterns of work and leisure, gender, and how the use and analysis of personal photographs have altered in line with scholarly approaches to history and memory (see Holland 2009; Spence and Holland 1991; Slater 1995).

Personal photography has diversified from the expensive and, to some extent, difficult production of single images during the nineteenth century, through the mass production, distribution and consumption of 'snaps' throughout the twentieth century, to the apparently infinitely expanding and diverse personal images people instantaneously produce and consume in the twenty-first century.

Early forms of personal photography between the 1840s and the 1880s were located mainly within the middle-class home and consisted of portrait images of idealized Victorian domesticity and military or exploratory travel. To be an amateur photographer – or a 'hobbyist' – to have one's family represented, to have the means to obtain private images or capture the 'exotic' of faraway places (related to the new practices of tourism and travel) for collecting and displaying purposes, were all conditions of privilege and, to a certain degree, wealth. Plenty of amateur photographers were women, but only those with relative wealth and domestic servants to allow for such a new leisure pursuit. Many of these aspects changed at the turn of the twentieth century as a result of new technologies of the camera, changing expectations about visual imagery, and the emergence of consumerism as a distinctive way of living in the West.

Whether through the postcard or the ability to pay for pictures in instalments, the turn of the twentieth century saw a rise in less advantaged socioeconomic groups being able to do personal photography and therefore engage in new forms of self-representation (Wells 2009). The forms such photographs took ranged from the apparent realism of the sporting event or working conditions to the staged portraiture in which people were placed against 'exotic' backgrounds. The emergence of *mass* forms of photography – made possible by the launch of the Kodak camera in 1888 – had a huge impact on who was able to do personal photography and precipitated the very idea of 'snapshots', through which many more people were able to develop their own forms of informal personal photography, often derided as being devoid of technical knowledge and skill. This, in turn, reinforced a distinction that continued throughout the twentieth century between 'personal' (frivolous) and 'amateur' (serious) popular photography, both of which have remained distinct from professional or 'art' photography. These distinctions also remained gendered: personal photography and practices of album-making were positioned towards women, while serious amateur photography, alongside professional and art photography, were dominantly framed as 'masculine'.

During the twentieth century the broader forms of popular photography proliferated through postcards, the mass production of photographic prints (which could incorporate personal portraits), and the use of photographs in rapidly expanding popular media such as newspapers, magazines, and so forth. Practices of personal photography also expanded and diversified, particularly in relation both to tourism and new modes of travel (car, rail, flight) and to the widespread adoption of the family album as the preferred mode of representing or, indeed, 'producing' the family. The largely Kodak-inspired association between personal photography and memory, developed at the turn of the twentieth century, became established and normalized across social classes during the 1950s and 1960s, as rising prosperity and the domestic economy became important locations for new ideals of family life and consumption. Images of Christmas, birthdays, holidays, and so on, became the standard stock of the family album, while at the same time idealized images of home and of family circulated more frequently within the burgeoning forms of popular entertainment, especially television and an expanding magazine industry.

In what might broadly be described as a continuing

democratization of personal photography, during the late twentieth century, practices of album-making and personal photo collecting expanded to include not only the family but, more often, friends and broader social networks, and also individuals themselves. The individual use of cameras within family arrangements became more common, as did the acceptability of personal imagery across popular media (e.g., as an aspect of celebrity culture). The emergence of digital photography at the level of the ordinary consumer during the 1990s transformed this landscape of personal photography in many different ways, extending the distribution of the personal or private image into a range of public spheres and global media.

The advent of personal photography, as one of several new visual technologies of the nineteenth century, is itself embedded within changes in visual mediation across Western culture. The ways in which new visual techniques were understood in terms of truth and fantasy, evidence and authentic representation, will be looked at in more detail in chapters 2 and 3. The emergence of new visual objects – photographs – precipitated new practices of collecting and organizing perceptions of the domestic sphere and the outside world. The ways in which photographs have been valued as material and symbolic objects has also shifted over the aforementioned period, bringing into question whether the digital photo can be valued as a durable form of self-representation.

This expansion and diversification has been made possible by technological change at the level of photographic industries in general, alongside specific developments in consumer-level cameras and processing techniques aimed at 'simplifying' photography (see Slater 1991). As will be explored in chapter 4, there have been comparable instances of significant technical change throughout the history of personal photography that have altered people's perceptions of what photography is and is for and who can do it, and have reconfigured what has counted as photographic skill and expertise. In this way, the actual activity of doing personal photography as well as the visual content it has produced will be considered in greater depth throughout.

Such technological developments make sense only in the contexts of late modernity and consumer capitalism. Many of the apparent certainties of the nineteenth and twentieth centuries represented within personal photography – the stability of family, employment, selfhood – can now be seen as ideals rather than realities, but they have also shifted in terms of being *dominant* ideals. Throughout the history of personal photography, 'the domestic' has been reshaped as part of processes of individualization in Western culture, the rise of 'identity' as the dominant category of self-consciousness, and the emergence of 'leisure' as a series of consumer practices in their own right. The ways in which, for example, memory practices have become commodified and tied to the consumption of technologies is of particular significance for the ongoing evolution of personal photography (see chapter 5). *Personal* photographies have not simply expanded, but have evolved within the wider field of photographies that have, in turn, been undergoing significant change.

Why ubiquitous photography?
Although there have been previous perceptions that cameras are *everywhere*, it is certainly the case that there are more cameras in use and more people engaged in practices of personal photography than ever before. What is the significance of this? The ubiquitous presence of the camera changes what can be, and is, seen, recorded, discussed and remembered, making the visualization of public and private life bound up with relations of power, expertise and authority. Indeed, the current *ease* of making images in everyday life has recently made *personal* photography subject to state intervention in the name of the prevention of terrorism, at least in the US and the UK. For example, alongside the restrictions imposed on taking photos

of the police, the ordinary ubiquity and politicized practices of photography have taken centre stage in public protest:

> The protests during the G20 summit were a carnival of photography. If they achieved nothing else – and that seems likely – they showed how the camera has become startlingly ubiquitous, as ordinary a recording instrument as the ballpoint pen but infinitely more believed than any words in a notebook. (Jack, 2009)

The June 2010 G20 summit in Toronto became a comparably visual event, with cameras and cameraphones described as the new 'weapons' in the struggle between law enforcement, professional journalists and ordinary citizens. Each attempt to assert rhetorical authority over public understanding of the event – to control how events are visually mediated – creates a panoply of visual claims and counter-claims regarding the conduct of all those involved. In these cases, what we have seen is the increasing visualization of everyday experience – also including accidents, social disorder, and natural disasters – and debates about the relative authenticity attached to it.

Figure 1.1   Camera wars

There have been other visual controversies stemming from the reconfiguration of personal photography through digital media, such as the attempted removal of pornographic images from Facebook in 2008, resulting in the controversial deletion of images of breastfeeding, and the ability to locate images of people's homes through the online mapping technologies of Google Earth and Street View. The permeability of public and private visual domains remains at the heart of many of these events and debates, an issue that has pervaded personal photography from its inception. On the one hand, there has been a vast proliferation in the numbers of visual technologies and images circulating within advanced capitalist economies. On the other hand, intellectual discourses and popular responses to this increased visuality appear to reproduce familiar debates, from anxieties about visual intrusion and authenticity to celebratory accounts of democratization and creativity.

The decidedly relative term *ubiquitous* is used to describe the present for several reasons. Firstly, in line with what Lister (2007), Rubenstein and Sluis (2008) and van Dijck (2011) suggest, the digitization of photography has enabled the photographic image to become networked within a range of globally connected flows of information. In this sense we see a radical expansion of the photographic comparable to that observed in the late nineteenth century, with the similar sense that personal life is becoming increasingly visible and visual in orientation. Secondly, the proliferation of visual technologies has become a key aspect of digital culture more generally, where digital imaging and photography have become thoroughly *ordinary* accompaniments to communication and connection practices in daily life. It is no longer a question of *whether* digital imaging and photography will become widespread, but how to understand the significance of this phenomenon (van Dijck 2007). Thirdly, partly as a result of these processes, the critique and problematization of the visual have taken centre stage in both social theory and popular discourse and practice

(Jenks 1995; Sandywell 2011). In this sense, the politics of visual representation, from concepts of truth and deception to privacy and democracy, has become an increasingly significant domain of critical public dialogue, whether in the case of visual evidence for the legitimation of military invasion or the prevalence of *visual drama* among teens via the smartphone (Marwick and boyd 2011).

In embracing the term 'ubiquitous', then, I am not referring simply to images: I suggest that the discourses, technologies and practices of photography have become *radically pervasive* across all domains of contemporary society. This is not an argument for technological determinism. Such ubiquity does not mean that photography, as a specific modernist field or aesthetic or technical practice, has simply spread exponentially as the inevitable outcome of technological change. Rather, what has happened is that some of the components of photography – and there is considerable debate about which ones (see Elkins 2007) – have morphed and become woven into the fabric of information technologies and economic, social, political and cultural forms. The implication is that, while the proliferation and convergence of visual and networked technologies creates a potentially ubiquitous photoscape with significant consequences, the ways in which images are produced, consumed, distributed and interpreted are tremendously diverse. Photography may be everywhere, but *it is not everywhere in the same way*.

The ubiquity of digital images and technologies has, on the one hand, produced a standardized visual landscape, where the majority of digital images are ordinary and mass-produced and form the 'wallpaper of consumer culture' (Frosh 2003: 1). These are the images we simply do not notice but that form the visual architecture of popular culture and contemporary marketing. On the other hand, vast numbers of photos that may have a uniformly pixilated form are meaningfully produced, used and interpreted very differently among social groups and communities of practice. In terms of both standardization and

Figure 1.2   Abu Ghraib image circulation

interpretation, photos taken in the routine conduct of daily life can assume the level of ubiquity. This is not simply breathless technological hype. Controversy over recent images shows the many ways in which the 'new world of mediated visibility' (Thompson 2005) enables ordinary photos to become visceral and visible in unprecedented ways while remaining open to continual reinterpretation.

The most obvious and cited example of this is the now infamous case of digital images of torture and degradation taken by American soldiers at Abu Ghraib prison in Baghdad in May 2004. This serves as an (albeit horrific) illustration of several key issues arising in relation to photographic ubiquity. Firstly, Susan Sontag (2004) argued that pictures such as these exemplify a key shift in photographic practice from preservation to communication. These images were taken *in order to be* distributed among friends and colleagues rather than to be carefully stored in an album. The notion that digital photography is primarily a form of communication rather than of memory-making is an important yet contested idea.

Edwards (2006), for example, argues that these images were intended as 'private memorials', like much tourist photography, intended to be taken home as mementos. The distinction drawn between public and private is central here, particularly as it maps onto communication and preservation. As Silverstone (2007: 122) argued, 'here was the private erupting into public space. Secrets were broken and the underbelly of western imperial power displayed.' But perhaps the more significant point is that the digitization and networking of these images allow them to exist *simultaneously* as private mementos and publicly shared images. Secondly, the sheer mundanity of the digital image capture process is striking and jars with the dramatic visual content. In other words, the popular 'critical' notion that the ubiquity of digital photos automatically renders them banal, trivial or ephemeral seems misguided when taken to be a general condition. Thirdly, the realism of these images has rarely been questioned. Despite the ongoing concern with the modified visual landscape of ubiquitous photography, exemplified in the term 'photoshopping', it is clear that the diverse circumstances in which relationships between digital photos and different modes of representation are enacted and accepted require empirical exploration. Finally, the modern distinction between professional and amateur photography seems anachronistic in an era when the most ordinary of everyday snapshots become the most iconic portraits of twenty-first-century politics (similar issues have arisen in relation to events such as the London Tube attacks the UK in July 2007, where the grainy amateur images have become the established account). In this way, what counts as 'amateur' or 'professional' has changed substantially. In the case of one set of images it becomes immediately apparent that the digitization of photography involves elements of social, technical and political novelty and convention that are difficult to tease apart and are certainly unpredictable in their affects.

The recent proliferation and diversification of digital imaging and photography prompts us to ask questions about the shift from analogue to digital. What has been the role and significance of photography in modern culture, and what are the historical continuities and discontinuities between film and digital photography? Is there anything distinctive about the digital turn in relation to photography? What kinds of theoretical and analytic approaches are required adequately to understand the implications of digital photography? What difference does technological change itself make for how people do photography and for what we consider as photography? How might established ways of image-making, organization, storage, interpretation and display be changing? What challenges does digital photography pose for those studying media and communication?

Photography and digitization

Photography's fundamental concept has been about light imprinting an image at a specific juncture in space and time. Digital imaging breaks the customary prescription by giving image-makers authority not only to determine place and time but to control space and time. This is possible because images are formed into a binary numerical code that is electronically stored and available for future retrieval (Hirsch 2000: 470).

In many respects the expansion of photography is a story of technological change over the course of the twentieth and into the twenty-first century. One of the most obvious indicators of major change is the almost complete disappearance of film-based technologies and their replacement with digital technologies. This by itself invites us to reflect upon the significance of film during the twentieth century, at the level of industry and employment, practice, aesthetics and craft, the iconic images in the popular imagination, the established ways of documenting and remembering, and so on. It is also evident that there are important challenges to the theory, institutions and practices of photography. The decline of film

– a technology so central to our understanding and experience of the twentieth century – is a dramatic event involving the disappearance of major institutions, forms of labour and employment, material infrastructures, skills and expertise, and specific instantiations of truth and memory. But such a transformation need not be interpreted in a deterministic manner. In recognizing the complexity and contested character of film photography, there must be a note of caution in producing a simple analogue-to-digital narrative, where social and cultural practices are driven by technological change.

What is digital photography?

An initial difficulty of accounting for substantial change is coming up with a rigorous definition of photography in order to provide a comparative context. Any definition of photography employed seems to raise as many questions as it answers. According to the critic John Tagg (1993), photography cannot even be defined as a medium, as the multitude of forms it takes defies reduction to a definitive set of specific technical characteristics or objects. The difficulties of establishing a consensus on what defines photography present the same problems in thinking about *digital* photography. Most commonly, this is understood to involve the technical difference of making the image itself. But even this is subject to debate. As Bate (2009: 155) has recently argued, 'Light is still registered on substrate materials, "captured" by light sensors, pixel receptors, rather than chemicals.' In other words, there is significant difficulty in isolating here exactly what it is that is continuous and discontinuous between film and digital. The film/digital distinction is pushed to an extreme by arguments that contend 'digital photography simply does not exist' (Manovich [1995] 2003: 240), meaning that, if there is no perceptible difference between analogue and digital images at the level of ordinary experience, no discernible category of 'digital photography' is plausible or useful. Throughout the book I argue that the distinction between analogue and digital is indeed problematic in many different ways – at the level of images, technologies and ideals – but that it is not simply to be dismissed. On the contrary, *how* the distinction is produced, enacted, contested and understood across different domains of social and cultural practice is rich territory for understanding just what might be meant by 'digital culture' (see Hand 2008).

Others exploring the relative continuity and discontinuity of digital photography have argued that the 'new photography' has rendered older debates about visual representation and power redundant (Van House 2007) or have shown how many of the established conventions of analogue photography are remarkably persistent through digitization. As Martin Lister has continually observed, we should be cautious about proclaiming a simple 'end of' story here. In contrast to several pronouncements during the 1990s of the 'death' of photography, 'digital technologies have not brought about the death of photography – there is more and more photography' (Lister 2007: 272). Technical processes of digitization have not simply eradicated, replaced or replicated analogue photography. The digitization of photography enables its current ubiquity as part of broader socioeconomic, technological and cultural changes associated with information societies (cf. Castells 2010; Lash 2002; Mosco 2009; Thrift 2005). At the same time, it is very much a part of the *everyday fabric* of social practices (Dant 2005; Miller and Slater 2000; Shove et al. 2007). In following this, I argue that, in principle, digitization is just as likely to reproduce aspects of film photography as it is to disrupt them. In other words, the digitization of photography involves elements of continuity and change in terms of how *images*, *technologies* and *ideals* are being reconfigured discursively and in practice.

In terms of images, there was much talk during the 1990s of the emergence of a 'post-photographic' era, based upon the notion that digitization would herald the disappearance of older technologies of visual culture and all the modernist values of truth and indexicality that came with them (see Lister 1995; Mitchell 1992). The rise of the photographic image during the twentieth century was inextricably tied to the growth of advertising and mass cultures of consumption. In this way, digital images are bound up with the changing visual face of capitalism. As Schroeder states, 'The current market revolves around the image, consumers consume visions of a good life, fueled by consumer lifestyle images' (2002: 43). It is now a commonplace to describe contemporary society as 'consumerist' or a 'consumer culture' (Dunn 2008; Lury 1996; Sassatelli 2007; Slater 1997), and in several important ways visual culture and consumer culture are treated as one and the same within theories of visual culture. With the shift from analogue to digital images, discourses claiming a 'break' with modern visual culture have emerged alongside practices that treat new forms of image production and consumption as photo-realistic.

In terms of technology, the expansion and proliferation of photography has been theorized as the outcome of broader systematic technological change, from modern mass production to postmodern flexible accumulation and now to global information networks. It is tempting to think that the practice of photography was in some way restricted by its analogue components, that it is has flourished as a direct result of digitization. This is partly true – new technologies change what it is possible to do – but the ways in which some of the cultural conventions of photography still hold sway suggest that technology and practice are *mutually constitutive*. Indeed, the idea that old technologies and their social relations are replaced by new ones has been subject to much critique (Bijker 1995; Latour 2005; Shove et al. 2007). Technical or culturally deterministic positions are often the outcome of inadequate accounts of both technology and consumption (Silverstone et al. 1992). Invariably, technology is taken as a self-evident series of artefacts, and consumption is defined as individualistic or mass acquisition as opposed to collectively in relation to social practices (Dant 1999; Warde 2010). There is no doubt that digital technologies are different, both materially and discursively, but the ways in which this is so depend upon their embeddedness in practices.

In the case of ideals, for the purposes of analytic clarity we might think initially of the cultural aspects of photography as those ideals and conventions – aesthetic, performative, skill orientated, ethical – that discursively shape and position photography as a distinctive and diverse practice of imaging. This is then an issue about the relationships established between ordinary practices and institutional arrangements, but also between cultural conventions, technologies and materials. Why and how is it that specific conventions of genre, scene, light, situation, subject, and so forth, have remained intact after digitization? What is it that holds these in place, what engenders change if it is not simply a technical or visual matter, and to what extent can this be observed in the shift from analogue to digital? This encompasses the actual ways in which people deal with film and digital photographs as material objects and involves how the specific photographic conventions related to aesthetics and performance become coupled and uncoupled to the social role and ethics of images. This includes not only lofty accounts of ethical images but also grounded sociological questions of how convention and change might relate to social structures and forms of life – family, class, gender, age, ethnicity, and so on.

A note on method

The research for this book drew upon a wide range of scholarly literature associated with photography studies, art history, archival theory, the sociology of consumption, science and technology studies, and new media theory. The empirical research took a number of forms between 2006 and 2010: archival research, content analyses, in-depth interviewing, and attendance at photographic trade shows and expositions.

These multiple methods stem from the theoretical and empirical concerns I have expressed about the need to take the histories of photography seriously while at the same time exploring the nuanced practices of making, storing and sharing digital images, without assuming that these are necessarily continuous or discontinuous.

Archival research conducted at George Eastman House, Rochester, New York, and Library and Archives Canada, Ottawa, on the emergence of digital photography involved several components. The first was a content analysis of a complete run of *Popular Photography* (1937 – present) and *PC Photo* (1997 – present) related to the emergence of digital photography as a recognizable practice, in terms of both institutional and everyday (or amateur) practice. Advertisements, editorials and articles were examined in order to identify and track key moments of change in representations of what *doing* digital imaging and photography involves and requires, which skills and new knowledge are necessary, the assumed benefits and problems, who it is aimed at, and what the appropriate contexts or subjects for digital photography are (e.g., family, tourism, events, people). The second element was a more focused investigation of the 'career' or 'biography' of the digital camera itself (Kopytoff 1986), tracing dominant trends in technical features, allied technologies and anticipated functions, drawing upon the above resources in conjunction with a range of market research data on camera development and acquisition, available through InfoTrends, the Photographic Historical Society of Canada, and online magazines such as *Digital Photography Review*. The utility of this work – deliberately relying upon photographic and computer-orientated sources – was to situate the development of key technologies and associated forms of knowledge and practice in broad sociohistorical context and to locate current technological innovation, consumption and use with reference to the changing status of imaging and photography in society. The aim was to pinpoint and track some of the trajectories involved in the coming together of current images, technologies and practices which are discussed throughout the book.

In-depth interviews with four specific groups were conducted in order to explore current constellations of belief, technologies, and practice influencing patterns of consumption and use. Each group was designed to focus (in principle) around a different aspect of digital imaging/photography: archivists and curators; members of a well-established amateur photographic society; undergraduate students; and residents from different areas of a local city. As well as investigating different forms of convergence between technologies (such as cameras, PCs, printers, email, photo-sharing sites), interviews were designed to reveal current *variations* in the ways in which people use these technologies. This included whether and how understandings of digital photography vary among social groups and societal levels, and how the substance, meanings and purposes of digital photography are actually being assembled and reproduced. While this book is not solely an exercise in disseminating new research, all the above materials are drawn upon throughout the book to provide substantive evidence or original illustrative examples.

Overview

I have suggested above that analogue and digital photography have aesthetic, economic, sociocultural and technical dimensions which position them at the intersection of several theoretical traditions and perspectives. Chapter 2 asks how the current proliferation of photography can be understood through theories of visual culture, consumption and technology. I show how elements of digital photography relate to recent thinking across the fields of sociology, media and communications, and science and technology studies. The key debates in this chapter are about continuity and change and question to what extent the digitization of photography disrupts dominant theories of visual culture, consumption and technology in late modernity.

Chapter 3 deals with whether digital images are qualitatively different from film images. The chapter provides a concise history of the photographic image and the photograph, drawing upon well-known scholarly literature and archival materials. Periodic shifts in the processes of image-making (daguerreotype, dry plate, wet plate, etc.) have been accompanied by different ideas about the changing status of the image in relation to culture. Alongside clarifying the technical differences between various film and digital images, the chapter discusses the central cultural implications of images as they become digital information. Three specific issues stemming from the new materiality of the digital image are addressed. Firstly, in contrast to the 'age of mechanical reproduction', we now experience a situation of infinite *variation*, with further implications for notions of aura, originality and authorship. Secondly, while photographic images have always been available for and subject to *manipulation*, malleability is implied as an unavoidable characteristic of digital photography, raising questions about how authenticity is understood and practised and how this may be shifting as part of wider cultural change. Thirdly, the cultural value of the photographic image as a *durable* material artefact has been contrasted with the idea that digital images are ephemeral or transient. They can now be viewed immediately and deleted, altered, distributed, and so on, all of which have been related to a notion of cultural disposability and to what has been called a 'new aesthetics of the everyday' (Murray 2008).

In chapter 4, I argue that it makes as much sense to think of ubiquitous photography in terms of the pervasiveness of technical artefacts – cameras, laptops, cellphones and smartphones – as it does to think about the ubiquity of images. The chapter asks how and to what extent digital photography is driven by technological change. It focuses upon shifts in the technological apparatus involved in doing photography in relation to the agency of the photographer. It shows how approaches that focus exclusively on the nature of the digital image miss some important aspects of technological innovation and convergence in relation to what photographers are able and expected to do. Three kinds of reconfiguration are examined. The rise of digital cameras is discussed in terms of how they have automated many conventions of photography that were previously expected to be learned, such as framing landscape, lighting, portrait and night shots. The focus is upon the relationships between these technical features, the promises they seem to make available, and the ways they translate into practice. The more specific issue of how the relationship between digital camera and photographer is altering conventions of 'skill' and expertise provides a way of examining shifts in photographic agency, involving the rapid accumulation of pre-production skills and the development of digital post-production techniques. The categories of amateur and professional, producer and consumer are blurred as a result. Finally, two forms of technological convergence are discussed in relation to the reconfiguration of the chain of elements that make up digital photography. The digital camera has been inserted into an expanding evolving system of technologies, which alters what cameras are able to do. It has also converged with other devices such as the cellphone, again altering the possibilities of photographic practice.

Chapter 5 concerns whether digitization has changed how people store and organize their photos in relation to memory practices. Digital photography reproduces and transforms relationships between photography and individual and collective memory-making, in terms of both informational images and the burgeoning image-capture technologies such as the cellphone. This chapter initially revisits studies of album-making in the domestic sphere in order to ask what is different after digitization. A number of questions are posed. Firstly, how are digital images organized, stored, viewed and shared? Does the immediacy and disposability of the digital image change how it is positioned in relation to individual and collective memory? What is the significance of photo tagging and the publicization of private albums through websites such as Flickr and Facebook? The chapter explores practices of tagging and photo management in relation to shifts in the relative significance of software and new modes of classification. Digital memory is cheap, such that we *routinely* store vast amounts of digital data and thus appear to remember a great deal, both individually and collectively. New technologies also change what can be remembered, and how it can be remembered, with specific consequences for notions of permanence and authentic interpretation. The diversity of emerging online photo management practices demonstrate how trajectories of both preservation and communication are enabled and intensified through self-conscious distribution. Distribution involves the multiplication of images, their simultaneous dispersion and storage across a range of media and, most importantly, their ongoing potential for remembering.

Chapter 6 concludes by gathering together the key themes of the book, arguing that digitization has encouraged both an unprecedented proliferation of image-making and distribution – the ubiquitous element – but also a radical diversification of what counts as photography in contemporary societies. Photography now has many lives, each of which may be related, but all are part of different trends and may have rather different trajectories in the future. This has intellectual, practical and ethical implications, equally important for scholars of digital media and general publics trying to make sense of visual culture in the present.

CHAPTER TWO

Visual Culture, Consumption and Technology

Introduction

Daily life in advanced capitalist societies has become increasingly *visually* orientated, organized around *consumption*, and saturated with *technologies* of one kind or another. This presents several challenges in being able to locate photography as a specific object for analysis in the twenty-first century. In this chapter I engage with three broad fields of inquiry – visual culture, consumption and technology – to show how they can help to examine the continuity and change associated with digital photography from different angles. There are two modest aims here: to illustrate how the digitization of photography connects with several major themes in contemporary social theory and to place discussions about photographic practices within interdisciplinary approaches drawn from visual culture and media theory, the sociology of consumption, and science and technology studies. Key themes and ideas will be discussed in turn as follows.

Firstly, current trends in digital photography are part of longer-term dynamics in the development of modern visual cultures. Digitization has prompted the re-examination of established connections between reality, the photographic and representation in ontological and epistemological terms. There are several key dimensions to this, from the association of vision with objectivity and truth, the pervasiveness of photography as an ideological formation, and the sociological relationships between power and visibility. Debates about the visual in modernity treat photography as an instrument that captures the real, but also deconstruct such a view through the critique of photographic truth as a mode of representation that is linked significantly to power. After digitization, it is arguably the case that modernist ideas of fixity, permanence and capture are giving way to notions of mobility, ephemerality and performance.

Secondly, the sheer prevalence of photographic images in society is tied to changes in the nature of capitalist production and consumption. In the context of consumer culture, the ongoing development of photography is the outcome of structural changes in capitalist modernity related to advertising and the promotion of novelty, as well as the increasing commodification of images and popular consumer goods. The field of 'visual consumption' can be approached along two main axes: either a tradition of critical theory that focuses upon the implications of commodified images in advertising or sociological theories of consumption that stress the diversity of ways in which photographs are made and used in relation to social practices.

Thirdly, the apparent dominance of technologies in everyday life, of which photography is but one example, is a key characteristic of contemporary society and culture. The digitization and networking of photography can be approached through theories of digital culture and information in new media studies which locate the proliferation of images within dynamic networks of information that are changing what is considered 'social'. The connections between digital photography and technological culture more broadly can also be explored through science and technology studies, which challenge some of our core theoretical assumptions about context and agency in relation to technologies.

Modernity, visibility and transparency

It has been argued that photography produced 'the array of mobile signs and images which constitutes the visual culture of the late twentieth century' (Urry 2000: 87; see also Lury 1992, 1998). Images are produced, commodified, made public and circulated on an unprecedented scale such that much of social experience is *visually mediated*, whether in the consumption of news or simply engaging in conversation, constituting a 'new world of mediated visibility' (Thompson 2005: 31; and see Silverstone 2007; Thrift 2005). As the visual becomes more central in digitization, relationships between the visual and notions of objectivity, ideology and social order have been subject to considerable academic analysis, in the fields of medicine (Kember 1995), journalism (Ritchin 1990), field science (Meyer 2008) and neuroscience (de Rijcke 2010), among others. The more specific debates concerning the materiality of the (digital) photograph itself will be discussed in chapter 3, whereas here I want to map the broader accounts of photography in visual culture as a means to situate the significance of digitization within social theory. Has digitization appreciably altered the relations between photography and a broader visual culture? Do we see, look at and interpret the world differently through digital means?

As an aspect of visual culture, the digitization of imaging has been largely understood as extending dominion over the visual developed earlier in modernity (Robins 1991); as radically undermining this specifically modernist understanding of vision stemming from the enlightenment (Mitchell 1992); and as both reproducing *and* disrupting aspects of modern cultures of vision (Kember 1998; Sturken and Cartwright 2008). Common to these different perspectives is the notion that the development of photography has been central in establishing dominant ideas about how images and reality are connected, and that radical change in photography implies shifts in these connections across the social field. The key questions are whether the connection is conceived as an ontological, epistemological, cultural or technical one and to what extent there has been radical rather than incremental change (Lister 1995). This in turn has implications for how specific visual cultures – global, state, institutional or familial – create order, perform classification, and enable and constrain how people are visually represented and understood.

The increasing prevalence of the visual in society is a central theme within broader social theories of modernity and cultural change, as well as of debates about the postmodernization and informationalization of culture. This signals the 'visual turn' in contemporary social theory (Jay 1993; Sandywell 2011), incorporating both an increased recognition of the significance of visual phenomena in society and more sustained theoretical reflection on the visual metaphors that have been employed in making sense of modernity. I will discuss both of these aspects below, as they help us to understand the significance of photography in social theory and how digitization affects the relationship between the two.

Photography and objectivity
There has been an ongoing debate about the ways in which photography can depict, mystify, construct and codify the real world. At the outset we can distinguish between different genres of digital images and their attachment to the real. For example, within the medical profession there is great concern that digital imaging *should* be able to depict the objective truth (de Rijcke 2010), as digital scans become routine aspects of neuroscience and prenatal observation. Similar issues arise in law enforcement (the popular crime show *CSI* is inconceivable without digital cameras) and, of course, journalism, as it becomes increasingly visually orientated and networked. However, within fashion, advertising and marketing the malleability of digital images is taken for granted and celebrated as part of the creative process (Frosh 2003). Concerning personal photography, while photos may be routinely cropped and adjusted using standard photo software, they are generally treated as documents of reality – they have a practical 'ontological realism' in this sense (Slater 1995: 222) – where it is hard to imagine questioning the nature of every image

we routinely encounter. In social theory and intellectual criticism, the nature of this relationship between the real and its photographic representation has remained contested since photography emerged. It is therefore important to understand how the connections between photography and objectivity were *stabilized* in the first place and why they are thought to matter.

Early forms of photography emerged during the nineteenth century in tandem with changing visual rhetorics of seeing, meaning and interpretation which treated the photograph as 'quoting' reality (Berger and Mohr 1982; Crary 1991; Sandywell 2010; Tagg 1988). This is partly to do with emerging scientific practices, broadly speaking, and dominant philosophies of science, nature and empiricism that sought to establish *causal* relations between nature and visual evidence (looking through a microscope, for example). In this sense, the digitization of images has taken place within a cultural framework that has historically positioned photography in terms of its relation to the empirical:

> The camera was invented in 1839. Auguste Comte was just finishing his Cours de Philosophie Positive. Positivism and the camera and sociology grew up together. What sustained them all as practices was the belief that quantifiable facts, recorded by scientists and experts, would one day offer man such total knowledge about nature and society that he would be able to order them both. (Berger and Mohr 1982: 99)

This association between photography and the dominance of *realist* social scientific thought has been well documented (Lister 1995; Sekula 1989; Tagg 1988). Although diverse in practice, pre-digital forms of photography were unavoidably bound up with specific conceptions of objectivity, realism and representation, authenticity and authorship that have to some extent constructed the parameters of theoretical debate about the significance of digitization in disrupting these. Lister's (1995) definitive essay on the ways in which debates about digital images have resurrected older ideas about photography shows how realist theories of the image (in which the image *denotes* the real) have become even more firmly attached to analogue photography, with constructivist theories of the image (in which the image *constructs* the real) most often used to make sense of the digital. A brief explication of photographic realism is required here, because it still serves as a problematic reading of analogue imaging and also of many genres of digital imaging at the present time.

Perhaps the most important idea here is the notion that photography could provide *unmediated* access to reality. This rests upon underlying conceptions of the ontological nature of images and the epistemological claims that can be made as a result. The ontological question – what *is* a photograph? – opens up a complex arena of philosophical problems concerning the relationship between light and its impression, the temporal capture of a moment in nature, and what kind of *affect* such an embodiment enables (Barthes 1977). In realist thought, a lot of this complex debate has been reduced to questions of the technical processes involved – that the impression of light on a material medium (a plate, a roll of film, etc.) is incontrovertibly *what was there*. Such an idea makes analogue photographs 'traces', 'stencils' or 'records' of reality, by virtue of the mechanics of the process. While the emphasis has been on the technical process constituting a *causal* relation between image and reality, the mid-nineteenth-century photographies developed by Daguerre, Fox-Talbot and Niepce were conceived not so much as a technical inscription of the real but as its unmediated reproduction, without the aid of the human hand (Marien 1997). The ontology of the photograph (what it *is*) was expressed in terms of discovering nature and revealing things as they are: 'The most transitory of things, a shadow, the proverbial emblem of all that is fleeting and momentary, may be fettered by the spells of our "natural magic", and may be fixed for ever in the position which it seemed only destined for a single instant to occupy' (Fox-Talbot [1844] 1981: 40–1).

The fixing process described here, the physical imprint of

light reproducing a singular moment, enables the photograph to be associated with nature as much as technology, with the perfect capture of the real, and subsequently to become a significant element within scientific practice (in which experimental results are 'seen' and 'witnessed'). The ability to make nature visible and knowable in ways that the human eye could not positions visual technologies such as the camera as quintessentially modern instruments. While realist theories of visual technologies have taken several forms, the commonality is how the images are abstracted from the broader social, political and technical conditions of their production in order to have *an ontology* that places limits on their possible interpretations. As Sontag says, in the case of the photograph they came to be seen as 'miniatures of reality that anyone can make or acquire' (1977: 4) rather than as cultural inscriptions or translations of nature.

The realist conception that nature is imprinted onto the technical medium enabled analogue photography to be situated within a realist epistemology: the photograph changes what can be *known* about the world. Another way of putting this is to ask what photographic knowledge is, and how it might differ from other visual and textual ways of knowing. In early forms of photography, an adherence to realism distanced the photograph from the romantic subjectivity of the painting (Lister 1995), positioning photography as free from human intervention. This is entirely consistent with the burgeoning use of images *as evidence*. It is the assumed certainty of the technical process – the 'physical truth chain' of photographic practice – and the inherent qualities of the photograph that grant it such evidential power.

As we shall see in detail in chapter 3, at the level of theory, the advent of digital imaging is thought to have played a significant role in *destabilizing* these modern ways of seeing and knowing, radically questioning the objectivity or truth effect of the analogue photograph both in ontological and in epistemological terms. If the realism of the analogue image is constituted by technical means, and those means have changed, then digital photography has dismantled the modern epistemology of the objective photographic eye (Mitchell 1992). It has created new kinds of objects – digital images – that can be ontologically distinguished from analogue images. From this perspective it has been possible to cast the shift from analogue to digital photography as a definitive and decisive break in the ontology and epistemology of visual culture, whether for good or ill.

Photography and ideology

> What makes a photograph real is more than merely print and paper . . . what is real is not just the material item, but also the discursive system of which the image bears its part. (Tagg 1988: 4)

A more nuanced historically and sociologically orientated approach to understanding photography suggests that the reality of images arises discursively and is primarily ideological in form. The questions stemming from what is in essence a social constructionist position – whereby the dominance of particular visual technologies arises through social and cultural processes rather than the other way around – examine the *rhetorics of vision* that have shaped analogue and digital photography; they ask how these have come to be dominant and with what consequences. Objectivity is not something revealed by photography but is *constituted* through it in relation to different institutions and social practices, producing *preferred* ways of seeing. Barthes (1977) showed how the analogue image could have 'indexical' qualities – that it did indeed have a 'being thereness' because of the imprint of light – but that the assumption that this was 'natural' is itself a historically and cultural specific way of thinking about the visual. Photographs *appear* to be miniature versions of the real, without ideological content (Urry 2002), but this is precisely their constructed mythology. The many forms and practices involved in analogue photography were seen as integral to ideas of what was *modern*, especially in terms of the development of machines and devices for revealing and mastering nature, but also more aesthetically in terms of *modernism* as a set of cultural practices (Idhe 1995). The results of photography – photographs – are not simply depictions of nature but embodiments of ideological or coded ways of seeing the world shaped by powerful interests and reproducible cultural conventions (see Berger 1972; Tagg 1988).

In epistemological terms, this asks us to consider what broader knowledge regimes are in place that 'naturalize' what is seen. This includes the kind of scientific construction of nature above, but also the naturalization of the family, gender and class through the dominance of domestic portraiture and visual rhetorics of the good life in the twentieth century (Slater 1995), plus the more widespread dominance of the commercial culture industry (Adorno and Horkheimer 1972). The importance here is that changes in the technology of photography – including the shift from film to digital – are not *necessarily* disruptive, unless they are part of a reconfiguration of visual culture as a whole (see Mitchell 1992). In other words, photography has always been a myth-making practice, and so revelations about the constructed nature of image-making and consuming would seem to be continuous with the history of photography. The notion that images can convey a convincing account of the real world positions photography as a key ingredient in the 'politics of representation' (Hall 1997). For example, the production of a photographic image involves decisions about what is to be included in the shot, how this is to be framed, for what reasons, and so on, which are aspects of cultural convention that are often institutionally regulated (the standardized school photo being a prime example of this). Most well-known theories of photography go further and deal with broader issues of representation, in which the *very idea* of making an image is a political act. To take a photograph is seen as an act of 'capture' – an instantiation of power over others. The ordinary act of making a photographic image is an 'active signifying practice' in that, according to Sontag (1979), the effort to make an ideal image 'neutralizes' its realness. For example, this notion has been developed in relation to images of suffering and deprivation, to constructions of the family and chronology, and to the visual construction of 'the other', especially exotic places, which become knowable through scripted visual vocabularies that have the result of shaping the reality they are thought simply to depict (see Urry 2002).

In terms of the continuity of visual rhetoric, there are clear similarities between analogue and digital photography when they are described as *immediate*. In what can now be seen to be typical about advocates of new media, the analogue photographic eye would see what was true regardless of cultural values and forms. As Bolter and Grusin (1999) have argued, when media are new they tend initially to be framed as offering an unmediated access to the real (e.g., the 'live cam'). Indeed, one of the key discourses of digital photography among producers and marketers has been the immediacy of image production and the notion that everyday life can be captured *as it occurs*. The sheer number of mundane images available in web-based image banks might be cited as evidence of the increasing documentation of everyday life as a generalized cultural condition (Bauman 2007; Murray 2008; but see Sandywell 2004). Moreover, the sheer pervasiveness of digital images at the present time can be approached as a radical extension of the photographic eye – the insatiability of the photographing eye as a mode of seeing and capturing life (Urry 2002).

In terms of how analogue and digital are positioned differently, digital photography has often been theorized in terms of a shift to postmodernity and postmodern visual cultures in several ways. Firstly, many have suggested that a cultural shift towards the dominance of irony, playfulness and bricolage has reshaped the nature of visual culture away from notions of fixity and objectivity and towards pluralism, self-referentiality and the detachment of the visual from the real (Baudrillard 1988; Collins 1995; Mitchell 1992). Secondly, there has been a shift from modern mass media and culture towards decentralized communications media (such as the internet), with an accompanying blurring of such forms as news, entertainment, documentary and advertising in the 'mediapolis' (Silverstone 2007; and see van Dijck 2007). Thirdly, the certainty of universal scientific knowledge has been critiqued by new ways of thinking that privilege cultural relativism, contingency and particularity (Lyotard 1984). In terms of photography, Jameson's (1991) account of how it has as a result 'given up' attempting to represent things as they are, and has become self-referential, has been an important idea here in framing responses to digitization.

There seems to be an affinity between aspects of postmodern thought and tendencies in digital imaging that mirrors similar theoretical connections between poststructuralism and digitization more widely (Hand 2008). Both the technical processes (digital images can be constructed without reference to an existing object, detaching the image from any referent) and the pervasiveness of digital imaging (images can be produced, exchanged and manipulated across time and space through decentralized information networks) seem to exemplify many important aspects of a shift from modern to postmodern visual culture. Both illustrate Poster's (1990, 2006) critique of modernist conceptions of digital culture and the idea of passive audiences under conditions of ubiquitous media. Similarly, the pervasiveness and infinite variation of the digital image point towards Baudrillard's (1988) conception of simulation – that sign-systems now dominate all understanding, without recourse to any concrete reality. Many of the admittedly abstract ideas developed in postmodern theorizing have been employed to argue for a decisive break in modern visual culture, not necessarily caused by digitization but certainly exemplified by key aspects of it.

Visualizing modernity
Moving into more grounded sociological territory, the importance of the coupling of realism and photography, whether
technically or discursively, lies in the social processes it continues to legitimate. Over the last two hundred years Western
societies have developed and deployed a vast array of visual
technologies that have fundamentally shaped institutions
and practices of social regulation, classification and order.
One of the chief aspects of modernity in general has been this
increased importance of vision and visibility (Foucault 1984;
Urry 2000) potentially establishing a mode of visual domination (Robins 1991). This has involved two broad processes.
Firstly, that society itself is *made visible* through technologies
of documentation, survey and classification (Foucault 1984).
For Foucault (1977), the new institutions of modernity – notably the prison, school and hospital – involved an increase in
the visibility of the population through bureaucratic mechanisms of surveillance, themselves a necessary aspect of the
new modes of societal regulation characterized under the
rubric of 'governmentality'. Making subjects and practices
visible in this sense makes them amenable to government,
broadly construed as those agencies seeking to regulate the
conduct of populations. As Kember argues:

> In the nineteenth century the new technology of photogra-
> phy operated as a fetishistic means of social control based on
> the disavowal of a threat posed by one section of the society
> to another. Control was articulated and inscribed on the body
> by subjecting the isolated individual to minute and detailed
> forms of visual, textual and statistical surveillance and clas-
> sification. (Quoted in Lister 1995: 99)

Intimately tied to this is the notion of the 'gaze' in its
Foucauldian sense, referencing the rise of photography as a
central mechanism of institutional visual classification, especially through the modern nation-state and scientific practices
such as medicine (Sekula 1989). The discourse of objectivity
alluded to earlier prompted the use of photography within

various bureaucratic institutions as evidence, documenting differences between the criminal and the non-criminal,
and identifying the visual characteristics of the 'native', the
'abnormal' and whoever was deemed 'other' at the time. In
other words, late nineteenth-century photography was commonly used to establish *difference* in the constitution of society
through social regulation. The relationships between ontological and epistemological conceptions of photographic realism
are not technically 'given' or established solely at the level of
ideology, but have been shaped by the demands of ordinary
institutional practice. For example, Tagg (1988) has observed
that the specific epistemological legitimacy of the photograph
as a material artefact arose because of its cultural value within
positivist philosophy and associated institutions that *required*
visual evidence in order to function.

This link between visibility and power can be seen in contemporary accounts of ubiquitous visual media (Thompson
2005) and the exponential rise of digital surveillance as the
'new transparency' (Finn 2009; Lyon 2007). In both cases,
the visualization of everything raises questions about who
establishes the rules and conventions of vision and to what
extent institutional, corporate and state power is increasingly manifest through the management of visual culture.
This includes at the institutional level the installation of cameras in urban centres, but also the billions of still images of
everyday life available on the Web. In this sense, everyday
life, at least in the affluent global regions, appears completely *transparent* and available for viewing in one form or
another.

Here digital photography seems to *extend* rather than break
with several trajectories of modern visual cultures. This intensification of the dissolution of boundaries between public and
private, sacred and profane, legitimate and illegitimate, and so
on, has long characterized modernity in sociology (Giddens
1991). Ordinary life has been further penetrated by advanced
technologies of vision, exemplified by the exponential rise in

the use of photography as a *juridical* technology. We can see this in fields as diverse as sport, law, forensics, and so on, all of which employ digital stills to produce an image of objectivity and make definitive decisions. We are currently living in an era of unprecedented surveillance, which by definition takes a primarily visual form and has been a central constituent of modern society (Giddens 1984; Lyon 2001). The current logic of this involves the pre-emptive categorization of persons, processes of continual watching and being watched, but also performance in the commercial and sometimes ironic use of CCTV, reality TV, the prevalence of scanners, movies about surveillance, etc. (Lyon 2007). The panoptic gaze theorized by Foucault (1984) – where the many are watched by the few (e.g., CCTV) – has shifted to a scenario in which the many *also* watch the few in popular culture (e.g., reality TV).

The second process is the more focused prevalence and ordinariness of *visual examination* across varied social practices. While such practices also make society visible, the significance here is the ways in which forms of visual reflection have become *routine modes of experiencing the world* through myriad practices of looking (Sturken and Cartwright 2008). Urry (2000: 83), for example, argues that, during the nineteenth century, 'sight' became far more significant through the increased circulation of new visual commodities such as mirrors and, especially, photographs. The significance of this is the role of photography in the promotion of visual appearances over other forms of experience and its prominence within a broader privileging of the cultural value of *fixing and capturing* visual sensations, such as encountering scenery and representing events, family, childhood landmarks, and so on. The employment of visual accounts of experience is central to contemporary journalism in particular (think of how we consume the news), but also in the public understanding of science, the criminal justice and legal system, and the dominance of visual marketing. At the level of everyday experience, Urry (2002) has argued that modern tourism could not have existed without the invention of photography. This central insight can now be extended in relation to a range of contemporary routine practices – sport, music events, travel, anything involving children – in which visual documentation appears to take the *primary* role in the constitution of experience, memory and culture.

In line with this, Silverstone (2007) recently argued that, while modernity has been defined by the increasing presence of technology, visual media technologies have been the most significant recently in becoming *environmental* and therefore central to the management of everyday life. By this he means that media technologies now provide the infrastructural framework for the ordering of communication and information production, consumption and exchange. One way of putting this is that media used to be more obviously external – people would choose to watch TV – whereas now screens (smartphones, iPods, laptops, TV screens) are prevalent and to some extent necessary in a far wider range of ordinary activities (Hand 2010). So, the visualization of everything involves *multiple* dynamics of power and vision and of ordinary experience and sociality.

Both broad processes discussed above are made possible by more abstract ideas about the relationship between vision and objectivity (or 'truth' in a broader sense) developed in modernity. At a broad cultural level, then, the expansion of photography through digitization can intensify *and* challenge some of the major aspects of modern cultures of vision. The development of photography has occurred in tandem with the military, scientific and bureaucratic activities of the state and the corporation, all of which have utilized visual technologies in ideological and classificatory practices. The expansion of film and latterly digital photography has at the same time been important to the ongoing development of capitalism and to the development of consumer culture.

Capitalism, commodification and consumption

The rise and development of reproducible photography was not a culturally autonomous phenomenon but was part of the shift towards the mass production of commodities and the promotion of *consumerism* from the late nineteenth century onwards. The emergence of consumerism as a distinct way of living in Europe and North America took place during the period 1880 to 1930 (Slater 1997), when consumer activities became valued as practices of freedom and pleasure and consumer demand for new commodities required continual cultivation, mainly through advertising but also through changes in labour conditions (Smart 2010). Photography has had several significant overlapping roles here in becoming a major industry in its own right, in producing new commodities such as the camera and the photograph that have become inseparable from everyday activities, and in being central to the development of advertising throughout the twentieth century. Photographic industries are currently undergoing dramatic change, as the demand for and production of film has all but disappeared and digital technologies and related products now dominate the image-capture market that has grown exponentially. This does not necessarily entail the disappearance of film companies but their reconfiguration around new markets (for example, Kodak's foray into high-street printing kiosks and social media ready cameras). Accordingly, changes in the structural field of photography – from film to digital – can be understood in relation to shifts in capitalist organization more broadly. This applies to the rise of film and the photograph as both advertising tool and commodity (Frosh 2003; Slater 1983), to shifts from industrial to post-industrial models of technical and cultural production in photographic, computer and software industries (Gere 2002; Manovich 2001), to market segmentation and increased commodification in the field of image-making and processing, and to photographic representations of capitalism.

Visual commodification

One of the central processes in the proliferation of photography continues to be *visual commodification*: firstly, the use of photographs in mediating idealized images of marketable products (i.e., advertising) and, secondly, photographs becoming exchangeable products, partly as a result of the increased consumption of cameras across society (Crary 1990: 13). The German cultural critic Walter Benjamin bemoaned the rise of advertising and its use of the potentially critical form of photography, thereby transforming photography into a myth-making enterprise rather than a form of critique. In this sense Benjamin argued that photography in its commercialized form was in danger of simply replicating capitalism:

> The creative in photography is its capitulation to fashion. The world is beautiful – that is its watchword. Therein is unmasked the posture of a photography that can endow any soup with cosmic significance but cannot grasp a single one of the human connections in which it exists, even where most far-fetched subjects are concerned with saleability than with insight. (Benjamin [1931] 1979: 254–5)

So, the development of photography was not only allied to positivism in its philosophical or scientific sense, as discussed earlier, but was inextricably shaped by an emerging commodity culture (Tagg 1988). As Kracauer puts it:

> In nineteenth century France the rise of photography coincided with the spread of positivism – an intellectual attitude rather than a philosophical school which, shared by many thinkers, discouraged metaphysical speculation in favour of a scientific approach, and thus was in perfect keeping with the ongoing process of industrialization. (1965: 5)

In order to understand how photography became ubiquitous, it is necessary to situate several ideas discussed so far within wider changes in the nature of capitalism, especially in advertising and market segmentation and the practices of consumers. It is generally agreed that the dynamics of capitalism changed significantly over the course of the twentieth century. The overarching story is one of a shift from mass production – following the model of the Fordist assembly line – to flexible customization – whereby markets are increasingly segmented and goods *customized* through signs and symbols rather than predominantly through manufacturing (Harvey 1989; Lash and Urry 1994). These complex changes have been associated with, among other things, the decline of mass culture and the rise of individualization and lifestyle groups, plus increasing uncertainty, risk and ambivalence in forms of employment and social identities (cf. Castells 1996; Thrift 2005). These shifts establish a socioeconomic context for understanding digital photography in relation to consumer culture and point towards different ways of approaching the ubiquity of images.

The majority of critique in the field of visual culture that takes consumption as its focus – often called visual consumption – has concentrated upon advertising and its audiences. Consumer culture is often understood as or, at least, typified in terms of advertising. When semiotic approaches to the image are privileged (Barthes 1977; Hall 1997), current cultures of consumption are theorized as the logical consequence of the insatiability and irrationality of image consumption, particularly the mythic construction of 'need' and desire via ubiquitous photographic advertising (Sturken and Cartwright 2008). Social theorists have sought to critique visual advertising as having considerable psychological impact upon consumers, of organizing them into homogeneous mass groups, producing stereotypes of the gendered consuming subject (Buckley 1986; Sparke 1986), and even of forcing consumers to act against their own will and judgement (see Slater 1997 for a history of these accounts). The use of photographic images in advertising is a key aspect of how capitalism self-consciously seeks (not necessarily successfully) to *organize* the visual field; as Schroeder states,

'The current market revolves around the image, consumers consume visions of a good life, fueled by consumer lifestyle images' (2002: 43). In terms of visual marketing, individual and collective identities now appear inseparable from photographic images, with the instantaneous and *malleable* nature of digital photography exemplifying the immediacy and fragmentation of late modern consumer cultures (Bauman 2007).

Historically it has been argued that the world of goods has a 'photographic face' (Cadava 1999: 135), such that products are conceived *primarily* in terms of their visuality communicated through global advertising industries and 'image factories' (Frosh 2003). But the ways in which the relationship between images and products is organized and theorized shifted significantly over the nineteenth and twentieth centuries, related to changes in capitalism and theories of the image and the consumer. Briefly, where it was once thought that photographic images in advertising 'reflected' the properties or potential effects of the products, it is now apparent that images and ideas often *precede* or *replace* products in an explicit and self-conscious way (consuming the brand rather than a product, for example) (see Schroeder 2002).

The increased use of photographic images in commodity capitalism strips commodities of information about their production and imbues them with a range of cultural meanings that *mystify* the object (see also Barthes 1973). Complex combinations of text, sound and image are employed to 'encode' products with specific meanings (Hall 1997. Cultural meanings attached to products via photographic images might be emotionally charged and anthropomorphic, and most importantly become embedded in the object (such that, say, perfume becomes 'romantic', 'feminine', and so on). The ubiquity of images under discussion is related to the expansion and reorganization of capitalist forms of production during the twentieth century, leading perhaps in turn to the 'victory' of exchange value over use value. One of the key claims of post-Marxist critical theory has been that cultural industries, particularly advertising, have been able systematically to connect a seemingly infinite number of images (meanings) to commodities (Featherstone 2007). As discussed, both Baudrillard (1970, 1981) and Jameson (1990) saw this as key to the development of postmodern culture: a culture of depthlessness, where images have no necessary relationship to objects but can refer simply to other images or ideas. For instance, it has been argued that the commodified digital photographic image has the effect of removing any specificity of the image, of rendering *all* equivalent as exchangeable and autonomous commodities (Taylor and Harris 2005; Sontag 1977). After digitization there are so many photographic images, many of which have no apparent relationship to the real, that they become indistinguishable and impossible to make sense of within established frames of reference. The theoretical notion here is that a connection can be made between the increased number of photographic images in the world and the totalizing effects of exchange value over use value.

Others, influenced by postmodern theory, have focused upon the performative and ambivalent aspects of advertising in constructing the (post)modern consumer (Featherstone 2007; Lury 1996; Sassatelli 2007). Advertisers know that consumers *know*, so to speak. The simple positioning of products in relation to generic images and meanings will no longer suffice in a media-saturated digital culture where the efficacy and symbolic meaning of products can circulate rapidly and be subject to endless appropriation, oppositional readings, debate and diversification. The strategies and 'tactics' that consumers employ (Certeau 1984) in decoding images against their hegemonic meanings and appropriating them for their own purposes – strategies that were identified within the cultural studies of the late 1970s and the 1980s – have become an accepted facet of advertising cultures (see Lury 1996 on this). Furthermore, it is thought that the *possibilities* of image interpretation have altered dramatically because they are not encoded in the modern sense of representation, and that the contexts for decoding have also altered in global information culture (Lash 2002). This is to do with digitization and the *mobility* of the image becoming free of traditional moorings (for example, the predicted demise of billboard advertising via hand-held devices). It is also an outcome of broader shifts towards producer–consumer reciprocity, or 'prosumption', in how the relationships between producers, advertisers and consumers are managed, negotiated and experienced (Beer and Burrows 2010).

Ideological representations within this refashioned capitalism interpellate the consumer in terms of needing constantly to accumulate and discard objects in order to resolve contradictions between (meaningless) work and (pleasurable) consumption. As Zygmunt Bauman argues:

> The society of consumers devalues durability, equating the 'old' with being 'out-dated', unfit for further use and destined for the rubbish tip . . . The society of consumers is unthinkable without a thriving waste-disposal industry. Consumers are not expected to swear loyalty to the objects they obtain with the intention to consume. (2007: 21)

The use of photographic images in advertising is one the most tangible forms in which people encounter ubiquitous digital photography – a phenomenon central to current constructions of ideals about how to be a 'successful consumer'.

Consumers and consumption practices
The ubiquity of photography refers to its cultural pervasiveness within media environments and the visual construction of the consumer, but also to the enormous consumer boom in *doing* photography. The emphasis on photography in terms of advertising, which has dominated the literature, connects with a central issue in social scientific studies of consumer culture: the relative *agency* of consumers in relation to changing structures or modes of provision. Debates about the interpretive agency of the viewer in visual culture often mirror debates

about the role of the consumer in consumer culture. The extent to which 'viewing' or 'looking' is thought to be 'consuming' has become a central point of argument, related to increasing visual commodification noted above and to rising consumerism in late modern culture. In this vein, a key issue for studies of visual consumption is the extent to which we can rely upon research on advertising and related visual materials to tell us about consumption processes 'on the ground', the actual experiences and practices of consumers and the social contexts within which consumption takes place.

While it is arguably the case that studies of consumption have employed inadequately sophisticated models of visual media and mediation (see Jansson 2002), it is also the case that the broad field of visual culture has often positioned consumption in terms of de-contextualized commodity fetishism read from a semiotic analysis of advertising and marketing materials alongside somewhat popular representations of consumers and consumer culture. If the use of photos has become ubiquitous in advertising and branding, this tells us little about several aspects of consumption *practices* that are significant here. Firstly, although not a central component of this book, it does not help us to understand how photographic images are interpreted more fully, incorporating the role of consumers in making, interpreting and remaking the meaning of images. Secondly, it is not clear what the relationships are between the personalization of advertising through ubiquitous photography and the extent to which consumers identify with and embody individualized modes of consumption. Thirdly, how does photography as a social practice connect with the broader landscape of consumerism typified by and in advertising cultures?

The acquisition and use of objects such as photographs in everyday life has practical, experiential and symbolic dimensions (Sassatelli 2007; Shove et al. 2007). In analyses of visual consumption, the latter have taken on undue significance. This is partly to do with a continued emphasis upon 'conspicuous consumption' (Veblen [1899] 1953) that, by definition, tends to privilege the visible, as opposed to 'inconspicuous consumption' (Grunow and Warde 2001), which focuses upon the routine and invisible. In this respect, the sociology of consumption (as opposed to consumer culture) offers resources for identifying the social-structural and symbolic nature of the consumption and the *use* of new photographic technologies in relation to different social contexts (Bourdieu 1990a; Horst and Miller 2006; Warde 2010). In this practice-orientated field, it has been observed that the proliferation of advertising images increases the range of options available to consumers in terms not only of what can be acquired but also of 'who they can be' (Warde 2005). The paradox is that this makes the problem of 'making the wrong choice' ever more acute (Slater 1997). As self-identity is now inextricably tied to consumption practices (Bauman 2007; Featherstone 2007; Giddens 1991; Lury 1996), the role of images in advertising in creating both markets *and* 'active consumers' is central. Consumption here is taken to involve more than autonomous individual choice, demand or passive inevitability, and entail ongoing collective processes of definition, acquisition and use. For example, an emphasis on consumption as *uses* has been employed as a way of explaining how standardized technologies or objects (such as photographs) come to be revalued in counter-intuitive and unexpected ways (cf. Edwards and Hart 2004; Horst and Miller 2006; Silverstone et al. 1992).

In turning towards ordinary consumption, the pervasiveness and dynamics of photography can be examined from the ground up as a set of meaningful social practices. For example, the domestic sphere is an especially significant context in which the practice of photography has taken place (Slater 1995). Much of the research on photography and consumption practices has drawn upon the insights of Bourdieu's classic work on amateur camera clubs (1990a) in looking at how photographic consumption reproduces dimensions of class, status, gender, leisure and identity (see Hirsch 1997;

Pauwels 2008; Spence and Holland 1991; Slater 1995). Bourdieu showed how specific conventions and 'rules' were developed among most members that served to legitimate particular styles and practices of image-making. These were positioned against 'snapshot' photography and complemented the class aspirations of these social groups. By the 1960s cameras appeared so ubiquitous and photography so 'easy' that the latter seemed to have become boundless. Yet, as Bourdieu observed, 'it appears that there is nothing more regulated and conventional than photographic practice and amateur photographs' (Bourdieu 1990a: 5).

Following this focus upon practices of photography, the agency of consumers in the production and consumption of images has been approached ethnographically in terms of how the dimensions of class, gender, location and identity have shaped the parameters of choice and practice (Rose 2004; Ruby 2005). The continued importance of this lies both in the usefulness of paying close attention to the ways in which consumption practices are legitimized and conventions established and in providing a way of looking at how the 'digital turn' has taken place among distinctive communities of practice – for example, within traditional photography clubs, household settings, and online communities where many of these conventions are made visible through posted discussions and comments (see Murray 2008). The potential differences and relations between these form a significant dimension to understanding the variety of digital photographic practices as well as their ubiquity.

In sum, digital photography involves, among other things, the use of photographic images in advertising and marketing *and* the meaningful production and consumption of images by consumers. Moreover, one of the key characteristics of ubiquitous photography in the context of contemporary capitalism is the *reciprocity* between these two analytic dimensions made possible by advanced information technologies, where the expansion of capitalist forms of production involves increased reflexivity (see Thrift 2005). This is not less exploitative, or less driven by the maximization of profits, but in reflexive capitalism consumers are 'put to work', so to speak, in producing images for brand identities and products through affective and immaterial labour in their use of networked digital devices (Arvidsson 2005; Holt 2004; Ritzer 2010).

Networks, technologies and practices

In the theoretical trajectories and debates discussed so far, the role of technologies and other materials has been largely implied or at least taken for granted, whether it be the information systems through which images are articulated or the more specific relationship between camera and image, and so on. But if we look at how technologized contemporary culture has become, particularly in relation to networked digital information, then it becomes clear that greater theoretical attention needs to be paid to the dynamics of technology itself in visual and consumer culture. The pervasiveness of the visual and the consumption of photography have been made possible by hugely significant changes in the dominant technologies operating within society (Heywood and Sandywell 2011). For some new media theorists, the 'computerization of culture' has been radically pervasive and affective across the field of communication:

> the computer media revolution affects all stages of communication, including acquisition, manipulation, storage, and distribution; it also affects all types of media – texts, still images, moving images, sound, and spatial constructions. (Manovich 2001: 19)

Digitization enables the image to become simultaneously the vehicle, context, content and commodity in consumer culture (Lundby 2009), in which all cultural processes, including visual communication, are increasingly computerized whether we know it or not (Manovich 2008). Visible signs of this are the increasingly commodified yet participatory culture emerging through YouTube, Flickr and a variety of platforms for user-generated visual content (Gane and Beer 2008), inaugurating at the very least a blurring of the boundaries between cultural production and consumption (Beer and Burrows 2007). We might initially say that this is somewhat similar to the argument advanced earlier by Baudrillard (1981) and Jameson (1991), where in a sense products refer only to other products in a generalized system of symbolic exchange. But, according to recent research on informationalization, such abstract theoretical propositions have become *materially tangible* in everyday life, partly as an outcome of ongoing processes of flexible accumulation (Harvey 1990), but also because of the emergence of new kinds of visually saturated informational commodities such as smartphones, which 'act' simultaneously as things, spaces and networks (Beer 2009).

Several scholars in cultural sociology and geography have argued that there are developments taking place that contest the modernist distinction between technology and society, which in turn produce challenges for theorizing digital information technologies that are often thought to constitute an immaterial or virtual environment (Hand 2010). Firstly, the information-technological contexts within which visual culture is now enfolded are themselves impacting upon more domains of social life and, in the case of social media such as Facebook, Twitter and wikis, are increasingly shaping changes in the social practices of communicating, meeting, seeing, and so on (Beer 2010). Secondly, the expanding circulation of images as part of digital information flows (via databases, search engines, platforms, file-sharing) and the ubiquity of interconnected devices through which they flow (laptops, cellphones, smartphones, tablets) create significant problems for analyses of technological impact and social context (what is social about social media?). Thirdly, it has been argued that the *speed* at which such popular sociotechnical innovation occurs is faster and involves a greater degree of reciprocity than ever before (see Gane 2006; Lash 2002;

Savage and Burrows 2007). One example of this is the iPad, self-consciously marketed to be (re)invented *through its use*. It is thought that the dynamics of information technologies are reproducing modern forms of capitalist commodification and consumption but also producing novel forms of convergence, materialization and mobility across the social landscape within which photography is now embedded.

Technical and cultural determinism

One of the key questions within photography studies, particularly in relation to the digital turn, has been how to theorize the technology that in part constitutes the medium. The dynamics of change associated with 'information' or 'network' societies or the more specific processes of digitization have often been articulated as deterministic narratives of utopian promise or dystopian threat, in line with earlier accounts of sociotechnical change during modernity (Barney 2004; Castells 2010; Hand 2008; Hassan 2008). As Lister (2007) observes, initial responses to digital photography during the 1980s and early 1990s took this decidedly deterministic form, predicting the death of photography as chemical procedures were simply replaced by digital code for good or ill. Sweeping judgements such as these, whether positively or negatively positioned, now appear misconceived, as we see the exponential proliferation of images and cameras across all aspects of contemporary society in ways that are far from monolithic. While there are some dichotomous elements to this debate – between a causal technical determinism and a causal social constructionism – there are more nuanced accounts of the relationships between technology and practice within the literature. Lister (2007: 252) provides a subtle reading of these debates, arguing that, in light of the new information-technological environments within and through which photography is currently being enacted, we should 'write the technology back in'. But what do we mean by *the technology*, and how can it be theorized in relation to photography? Does it define the medium of photography? In what ways does technology shape the practices of photography, or is it the other way around?

There have been many important interventions that have challenged forms of technical determinism in accounts of media and technology, or photography more specifically. The majority of this critical thinking has rightly questioned the degree to which technologies can be theorized as separate from society or culture and other technologies, and, following this, that they can be identified as the *causal* agent of stability or change. This problem is neatly articulated by Lister in relation to photography:

> The dramatic 'impact' of digital technology on the production, circulation, and consumption of photographic images is being too easily seen as the impact of one singular and monolithic technology on another. Flowing from this, the social and cultural significance of the impact is being too readily read off from what are presumed to be the essential characteristics of the technology. (Lister 1995: 7)

However, it is equally problematic simply to replace technical with social or cultural determinism – to argue that culture determines technology rather than the other way around (see Latour 2005). While some interactionist versions of social or cultural constructionism (or 'social shaping') have become something of a default within cultural studies, mainstream sociology and communications (see Baym 2010, for instance), within science and technology studies and material culture studies we find different emphases on both the relativism and the rhetorics of technology (Woolgar 2002) and the performative relationality of technology and culture (Law 1994, 2008), each of which has implications for how digital photography is understood.

While there are several variants in science and technology studies, what they have in common is an attempt to problematize what essentialist theories take for granted as technology (Bijker and Law 1992), stressing that, in contrast to technological determinism, there is nothing *inevitable* about technological development or the effects of a technology (Bijker et al. 1987). Regardless of what looks retrospectively logical or linear, things might always have been otherwise. A central concept here is 'black boxing', through which the inner workings of technologies are invisible to users and society more generally: the properties and capabilities of a technology then appear self-evident or inevitable. But this is a social process, closing down alternative explanations or interpretations of the technology (Bijker 1995; Latour 2005; Sismondo 2009). Social constructionist positions attempt to show how technology actually emerges through complex negotiations between social actors, the outcome of which cannot be determined in advance, and in fact continues throughout the life of technologies, although this can be highly constrained by powerful interests. The histories, present and futures of any technology – in this case photography – are varied, multiple, contested and non-linear in practice. When technologies do become stabilized, it is the result of a social process rather than a progressive 'technical' development towards the most superior design, use or interpretation.

In some approaches, technology is conceptualized as rhetoric rather than as a social construction, in that it can never speak for itself or simply embody social interests. The claims for the inherent characteristics of either analogue or digital photographic technologies are just that – *interested claims* with particular agendas rather than objective descriptions – and this is no different whether it be from a manufacturer, marketer or cultural critic. The point here is to analyse the capacities and effects of technologies in terms of how particular accounts of both come to be persuasive and dominant and in what circumstances (Grint and Woolgar 1997). For example, this relates to the notion that the truth effects of analogue and digital photography differ in relation to the contexts in which such claims are made. This also leads us to examine claims of novelty made about particular technologies and how they may become convincing. This is a radical position that seeks to decentre technology as the discursive outcome of technical and non-technical elements in society. A third position, associated with actor-network theory or the 'sociology of associations', stresses the materiality and performativity of the technical in relational terms. For example, Latour argues that objects do not reflect the interests or claims of social actors that have been built in and black boxed, but instead have an *agency*: 'In addition to "determining" and serving as a "backdrop for human action", things might authorize, allow, afford, encourage, permit, suggest, influence, block, render possible, forbid and so on' (Latour 2005: 72).

The constructionism here is not social, as there is no sense in distinguishing between the social and the technical. Each can only ever be an aspect of the other, as there is no definitively social or technical stuff, only material out of which what we think of as society is continually assembled and reassembled. From the perspective of actor-network theory, while technologies can be said to have specific features, these only become manifest through use, which is itself situated within a broader sociotechnical arrangement: 'What is inventive is not the novelty of artifacts and devices in themselves, but the novelty of the arrangements with other objects and activities within which artifacts and instruments are situated, and might be situated in the future' (Barry 2001: 212).

Others have argued that technologies or objects have agency, in that they carry 'scripts' which enable and constrain the possibilities of action (Akrich 1992). For example, cameras are objects that carry inscriptions about their intended use. These might be prescriptive (cameras configure users to hold them) or open (cameras can make images of anything), but they are inscribed with the materiality of the object, not only descriptions of it. As such the camera has a level of 'interpretive flexibility' (Bijker 1995), but it is not limitless or only a matter of human interpretation. This immediately suggests that a great deal of specificity should be taken into account when we examine stability of change in relation to technology. The ubiquity of photography becomes a question of how such a complex assemblage of elements has become *stabilized* within such a wide range of environments from the ground up (Van House 2011). Such a question cannot be reduced to the 'truth-wielding' power of photography as a medium, the success of advertising or consumer capitalism, but has to be approached empirically in relation to the dynamics of practice (Shove et al. 2007). In taking a relational conception of digital photography, then, the analytic focus shifts to how technologies become configured with other elements to produce a recognizable *practice*.

Technology and practice

Digital photography can be approached as a technological formation that is both the outcome of practices and the material infrastructure of those practices. Building upon the notion of a 'heterogeneous network' or 'assemblage', the pervasiveness and diversity of digital photographic practices is explored from the ground up (Shove et al. 2007). There is nothing new about conceptualizing (digital) photography as a practice (rather than a cultural form, medium, technology or field), but recent developments in practice theory have incorporated the above insights from science and technology studies that allow for a rethinking of agency in relation to technologies and objects.

Don Slater's conception of photography as a range of material practices is an important one and serves as a conceptual starting point for considering what the elements of such practices are and how they have remained continuous or changed:

> mass photography is a range of material practices – practices set within developing social relations. Mass photography is integrated into the very fabric of the most intimate social relations (in particular, the family, leisure, personal remembrance and private vanity); is inscribed in institutions (from the photo press and camera clubs to high-street photographers and schools); and is bound up with the material conditions of consumption (relating to class, income, sex,

advertising and retailing, the ownership of the means of distributing images). (Slater 1985: 246)

In bringing together theories of visual consumption, technology and practice, digital imaging and photography are
theorized as *integrated sociotechnical practices* – practices which
combine discursive, material and image-based elements in
potentially different ways, framed by historically specific,
diverse interests and contexts. In contrast to theories of visual
consumption ,which neglect the specificity of consumption
practices, and theories of practice, which maintain an inert
model of technology, changes in the materiality of technology
alter the possibilities of practice, while the specific materialities of digital technologies are, in turn, shaped by situated
practices through which conventions become stabilized (Law
1994; Shove 2003). In following the formulation of practice
theory by Shove et al. (2007), photography is an abstract practice or entity and at the same time a grounded practice or
performance. In other words, we can refer to digital photography as a recognizable entity, albeit a vague and abstract one,
which is continually produced by the very acts of *doing* it in the
everyday performative sense. The importance of this is that
changes in *either* conception of digital photographic practice
have implications for the other. So, if changes occur on the
ground, such as the increasing use of cameraphones or smartphones to produce and share images online, then the more
abstract sense of digital photography is altered, which, in turn,
changes what people imagine themselves to be doing and how
new expectations are developed.

The technical characteristics of digital photography can
be said to evolve in tandem with shifting conventions and
practices of use (Oudshoorn and Pinch 2002) that remain,
at present, somewhat uncertain. While this might appear
straightforward as a proposition, the precise dynamics of co-
evolution are anything but. Even when technologies appear
stable – that is, when their design is fixed – their acquisition

and use remains a process of translation and invention, as their purpose and cultural significance is always on the move (Bijker 1992). This positions ubiquitous photography as a range of dynamic practices that weave together forms of visual commodification, consumption and technology.

Concluding remarks

In this chapter I have critically appraised a somewhat large and at times unwieldy body of literature in an effort to contextualize ubiquitous photography within a broad cross-section of ideas. The primary purpose has been to show how the digitization of photography, far from being a specialized field of inquiry, is related to a number of important debates about the significance of digitization within contemporary social theory. It is clear that the shift from analogue to digital imaging has been theorized dominantly in terms of the *intensification* or the *disruption* of processes developed in modernity. The digitization of imaging has to varying degrees been associated with major developments in visual representation and meaning, in the commodification and consumption of images, and in the technologies of visual representation and communication. The interrelations between photography and the apparent certainties of visual representation in modernity, of mass production and consumption, and of technological mastery during the late nineteenth and the twentieth century appear *reconfigured* by the ubiquity of digital visual technologies in networked cultures of consumption.

The secondary purpose has been to argue that, in order to think about how continuity and change in the field of photography might be approached from different angles, we have to bring together ideas and approaches from research in visual and media culture, the sociology of consumption, and science and technology studies. The chapter has acted as a survey of sorts but also as an attempt to establish a dialogue between diverse positions that will be pursued in the subsequent chapters. I have suggested that we have seen significant shifts in how photography is understood theoretically, partly as a result of shifts in the technologies but also in tandem with wider intellectual debates about realism, representation, ideology, consumption, and so forth, in the context of broader social and cultural change. I have suggested that there are trajectories within theories of information and in science and technology studies that have much to offer in conceptualizing digital imaging and photography as integrative sociotechnical practices. The next three chapters focus more specifically on stability and change in relation to the photographic image, the technologies and techniques involved, and the emerging memory and classification practices of digital photography, respectively.

CHAPTER THREE

Images and Information: Variation, Manipulation and Ephemerality

The photograph was formerly the representational medium under which all others could be subsumed, distributed, and analyzed. Today, that role must be allotted to the computer graphic. Under its domain, the photograph is transformed into being simply one among many representational forms. (Lunenfeld 2000b: 57)

Introduction

Most histories and social theories of photography have prioritized analyses of the photographic image over practices of photography, studying the discursive, semiotic and material character of photographs while paying less attention to how they are used. It is not surprising, then, that the digitization of photography has been approached primarily in terms of new kinds of images, asking whether they are qualitatively different from analogue images. In this chapter I will discuss the cultural implications of the translation of the photographic image produced by light-sensitive chemicals into the digital image produced by the conversion of visual information into binary code. Despite the attractive simplicity of this dichotomy, the nature, implications and significance of this shift from film to digital images have been subject to intense debate over time (cf. Kember 1998; Lister 1995; Mitchell 1992; Osborne 2010). Debates within the specific field of photography are significant in their own right – particularly the different ways that the relation between materiality and authenticity has been conceptualized – but they are also an important arena for

examining wider debates about the changing role of images in
contemporary society.

I begin by examining briefly the idea that analogue and digital images have different materialities and ontological status.
Three related issues are then considered. Firstly, the materiality of digital code enables the potentially infinite *variation*
of the image, with further implications for notions of 'aura',
originality and authorship. This has been discussed at length
since the 1980s, but the present pervasiveness and diversity
of ordinary digital photography brings the debate back into
prominence. Following this, while photographic images have
always been malleable, *manipulation* is implied as an unavoidable characteristic of digital code, raising questions about how
authenticity is understood and practised and how this may be
shifting as part of wider cultural change. Finally, the cultural
value of the photographic image as a 'durable' artefact has
been contrasted with the idea that digital images are necessary
ephemeral or transient. They can now be viewed immediately
and deleted, altered, distributed, and so on, all of which has
been related to a notion of cultural 'disposability' and to what
has been called a 'new aesthetics of the everyday' (Murray
2008). In each case I situate the debates historically, as the
issues raised here are not unique to digital images alone. It
would be a mistake to see so-called crises of realism, manipulation, reproduction, and so on, as emerging only in relation
to digitization, or even more simplistically as being *caused* by
it.

By drawing upon a wide range of sources, including interview material, I argue that, while the digitally encoded image
has challenged the *ideals* of analogue photography, in practice we find an *intensification* of longer-term problems in the
uses of still photography. Digital information takes a material
form, one that allows for the multiplication and diversification
of camera-produced images *and* the contexts within which
they can become valued, interpreted and performative. Rather
than ushering in a condition of debilitating virtualization, or

simply reproducing the documentary conventions of photo-realism, the translation of the photographic image into digital information has to be understood as potentially multiplying its material forms, each of which might have different relationships to their analogue counterparts. When explored on the ground, digital images may or may not be considered authentically photographic in the material forms they take and the contexts in which they are used.

What is a photograph? Materiality and meaning

Within the canonical literature, discussions of pre-digital photography have much to say about the different material forms it has taken, from Calotype to Polaroid, and how these have structured the nature of the image and its possible meanings (see Hirsch 2000). The notion of attributing some form of authenticity to the photograph is challenged by digitization. Some argue that the digital image is a radical break in the history of the photograph. For example, in media theory, Lunenfeld has argued that the primary effect of digitization is the displacement of the 'privileged real' of the formerly unique photograph, now merged with the 'overall graphic environment', which is malleable in form (2000b: 59). For others, such as Manovich's ([1995] 2003) earlier account of the 'paradoxes' of digital photography, technical change does not necessarily lead to any changes in the *practices* of photography, where people seem routinely to fail in distinguishing between film and digital images. The point here is that changes in the material form of the image are open to quite different interpretations.

The distinction between analogue and digital images is usually drawn in the following way: analogue images contain physical markers on their material surfaces – whether a painting or a photograph – that have a direct relation to the object represented (the gradation of tone representing light, for example). In this sense they are *transcriptions* of material properties. Digital images exist as binary digits of information, either 0s or 1s, sequences of which are usually called binary code or bytes. In digital cameras, light is also sensed in this way, but digitization refers to the almost immediate process of converting this visual information into code. In personal photography this includes the digitization of analogue photographs when we scan them or rephotograph them with a digital camera, or simply generate images using a digital camera. In both cases the digital code is detached from the material object, and can then be stored, accessed, altered, distributed and received in digital form through a range of devices and systems. Although both (analogue) transcribing and (digital) converting processes are translations of data, the original analogue photographic image is not separated from its material medium, whether plate or film. However, the digital image can start life in this form and can be converted and distributed through different media because of the *variability* of code (Manovich 2001). For some, it is this shift in *materiality* that marks digitization as a genuine rupture rather than just one of many evolutionary developments in the history of photography:

> Despite the difference between a daguerreotype and a Polaroid print, the photograph has always been based on a chemical process. Images are now being generated on the basis of electronic processes which fundamentally change the terms by which we relate to the photograph, retrieve, experience, and read it. (Clarke 1997: 218)

The argument here is that the relations between materials and images has fundamentally changed and, more importantly, that this alters our interpretive relations with images. But how did this association between materiality and meaning (not only image and objectivity) become so important in photography? Does the material change in the digital image result in a complete loss of *all* the assumed qualities of the photographic image?

Analogue and digital materialities

As we saw in chapter 2, during the mid- to late nineteenth century, debates about the advent of the photograph focused on the apparent realism of the image. Such debates took a technically neutral or deterministic form. For example, it was asked whether a photograph provides us with an accurate 'copy' of nature. This was exemplified by Fox-Talbot's notion of the *Calotype* image as 'the pencil of nature'. Here, the technology of photography is viewed as neutral, like a transparent mirror of nature, with an 'essentially objective character' (Bazin 1967: 13). The ability to produce an image without the drawing hand suggested an almost natural transparency to the photograph. This was because the photograph leaves few traces of the process of its manufacture – unlike, say, a brush stroke in a painting. The positioning of the photographer as human agent and the camera as non-living tool is integral; in order for cameras to do more than produce a transparent access to reality, the photographer would need to become explicitly creative. The notion that photography could or should operate as a neutral instrument was argued strongly by Baudelaire:

> Photography must, therefore, return to its true duty which is that of the handmaid of the arts and sciences, but their very humble servant, like painting and shorthand, which have neither created nor supplemented literature. Let photography quickly enrich the traveller's album and restore to his eyes the precision his memory may lack; let it adorn the library of the naturalist, magnify microscopic insects, even strengthen, with a few facts, the hypotheses of the astronomer; let it, in short, be the secretary and record-keeper of whomsoever needs absolute *material accuracy* for professional reasons. (Baudelaire [1859] 1980: 297; emphasis added)

The rhetoric of photographic technology as an instrument that materially 'fixes' its subject has many subsequent formulations. In the strong argument, the ontology of the photograph (its nature, not necessarily its *meaning*) is material in the sense that its realism arises *causally* through the successful transmission of light onto the object. According to Barthes (1982), regardless of human intentionality or institutional ideology, the analogue photograph fixes the reality of the scene through a continuous message. The image could not exist without the object in the external world; the image captures what is there. The process of transmitting the reality to the photograph is not literally seamless, but is continuous. In this sense, the photographic image is unique in its indexical relation to the photographed (Peirce 1955). While photographs can have many subsequent and parallel meanings, through reproduction, enhancement, distribution, and so on, there is an irremovable trace of the singular 'denotive' meaning *caused* by light and chemicals (see Barthes 1982). This strong account of materiality has formed the principal backdrop to the notion of a digital 'break' in terms of images. The basic idea is that the analogue image *necessarily* captures something real in its very material form, and this places technical limits upon its subsequent uses and 'connotative' interpretation.

There seems to be an immediate difference between this tactile chemical print and the largely invisible machinations of the personal computer. But the digital is often, and quite wrongly, equated with the *immaterial* (van Dijck 2007), which is then taken to remove any limitations for interpretation. For example, the physicality of the analogue image leads some to argue that the digital image does not, indeed cannot, have any claim or relationship to the real:

> Digitalization destroys the photographic image as evidence of anything except the process of digitalization. The physicality of the plastic material represented in any photographic image can no longer be guaranteed. For documentary to survive the widespread diffusion of such technology depends on removing its claim on the real. (Winston 1995: 259)

As Lister has argued, what is laundered from such a view is the *intertextuality* of all still photography in the first instance: how the photographic image has always been inserted within other contexts that have given it meaning; it is never 'met in isolation' (1995: 12). This is often recognized from an anthropological perspective, where the material/meaning of photographs has been the outcome of how they are *used* rather than how they have been made (Edwards and Hart 2004). Moreover, the apparent realism of the *content* of the image has always had to be manufactured through staging, framing and props. In early portraiture, the sitting subject of photography had to be literally stabilized by wearing clamps in order to remain still for the lengthy exposure times required to produce a daguerreotype (Berger 1972; Manovich 2001).

However, despite the long-standing critique of naive realist materialism – that the materials unproblematically *embody* and provide unmediated realities to the viewer – this remains the conventional standard to which the digital is compared. The most pervasive discourse of digitization more generally has been that of the immateriality of information, or what Hayles (2005) has called the 'dream of information': digital information is conceptualized as free of material context such that digital images represent a radical break with analogue. For example, according to Crary (1993), in contrast to the humanist conception discussed above, a 'virtual' or non-human form of vision is inaugurated through digital imaging. For Hayles, this conception of information is itself misleading in that information is always *embodied* within a constellation of structures, including 'the late capitalist mode of flexible accumulation; the hardware and software that have merged telecommunications with computer technology; the patterns of living that emerge from and depend on access to large data banks and instantaneous transmission of messages' (1999: 313).

The key point here, alluded to in chapter 2, is that digital information, like other inscriptions, is always embedded in materials and practices, albeit in different ways. Any novelty of digitization should be open to exploring *continuous and discontinuous materialities* rather than starting from the premise that information escapes context. An excellent example of this approach is Frosh's argument about the *polysemic* nature of the digital stock photograph. He argues that it cannot reveal intention, nor can its meaning be fixed, because it is 'polysemic and formally malleable *by design*' (2003: 73; original emphasis). Frosh shows how this in-built malleability is both material and discursive, taking the form of 'planned unpredictability' and necessarily offering multiple trajectories of codification and classification. The difference between the digital and the analogue here is a subtle one. As discussed above, Roland Barthes argued that, while the materiality of the photographic image entailed one kind of fixity in its singular *denotation* of the referent – showing something that was actually there – the *connotative* meaning – what this actually means – 'depends on the reader's knowledge just as though it were a matter of a real language, intelligible only if one has learnt the signs' (1982: 28). For Frosh, the polysemic nature of connotative meaning now occurs *prior to looking*; it is designed into the digital stock image in both its material form and its discursive rationale. However, whether talking about analogue or digital images, their subsequent *uses* are not necessarily implied or structured in the images themselves. There have been different ways of ascribing their material differences. Beyond the simplistic dichotomy of analogue materiality and digital immateriality there is an important debate about the extent to which the material variability of digitally coded images makes them open to limitless interpretation. That is, they can be continually inserted into multiple contexts, and therefore *remain* polysemic.

Reproduction and variation

One of the most important debates in studies of photography is how changes in the technical reproducibility of the photographic image alter the ways it can be viewed and interpreted and who is able to do this (Benjamin 1999a). There is nothing new about the reproduction and circulation of photographic

images, at least not since the 1880s (Tagg 1988). It is arguably the shift from mechanical reproduction (the production
of copies) to digital *variation* (the alteration of code) that
shapes the differences between film and digital images. The
ability to produce photographic images from a negative makes
mass reproduction possible, whereas the ability to remake the
digital image over and over again, and reproduce any of its
discrete components as images *in their own right*, challenges
the distinction between originals and copies (Frosh 2003).
Digitization radically changes the possibilities of reproduction and circulation as the image is detached from its *primary*
material vehicle, altering its status (it can be deleted), who can
view it (it can be networked) and how it can be interpreted (it
can be simultaneously received and altered).

The argument that new technologies of reproduction significantly alter the role of the image in society has been
continually drawn upon in relation to photography (Benjamin
1999a). Benjamin's argument during the interwar period was
that the reproduction and circulation of art objects enabled by
new mechanical means brought about the demise of the 'aura'
of a specific artwork, allowing for more widespread engagement and interpretation (as in the mass-produced fine art
print, for example). Benjamin argued that the distinctiveness
and authority of the art object's unique nature was fundamentally changed by mass mediation. This 'aura' of an artwork
cannot be reproduced because of 'its presence in space and
time, its unique existence at the place where it happened to
be' (1999a: 220). The authenticity of the art object is, then,
produced though its uniqueness and its location. Copies are
perceived as 'less authentic' than the original but with potentially democratizing effects, as the audience becomes larger
and more differentiated, and the individual spectator may
interpret the image outside of the 'ritualistic' and elite context
of its traditional display (e.g., a gallery). Benjamin recognized
that the democratization of the image from a unique or singular production might not necessarily be a positive scenario.

It could increase the possibility of oppositional readings but equally lend itself to the politicization of the *persuasive* image, a point he later makes about the conjunction of advertising and photography in popular culture.

While the mass reproduction of images in the twentieth century altered distribution and potential audience – by removing images from their original contexts and opening them up to simultaneous plural reception – the variability of digital code theoretically allows audiences to become individualized distributors or even producers, as a digitized cultural object can be customized at will. The spectators of Benjamin's reproduced image are exactly that – viewers. They may appropriate images for unintended purposes, and this is itself arguably a productive form of cultural engagement, but the object itself remains consistent. The difference between the reproducibility of analogue and the variability of computerized media forms is articulated in relation to industrial and post-industrial societies by Manovich:

> Numerous copies could be run off from the master, and, in perfect correspondence with the logic of an industrial society, they were all identical. New media, in contrast, is characterized by variability. Instead of identical copies, a new media object typically gives rise to many different versions ... Stored digitally, rather than in a fixed medium, media elements maintain their separate identities and can be assembled into numerous sequences under program control. In addition, because the elements themselves are broken into discrete samples (for instance, an image is represented as an array of pixels), they can be created and customized on the fly. (2001: 36)

In terms of the relationships between these changing technical conditions and meaning, I want to draw out two related lines of argument stemming from this observation that 'many different versions' of digital images are 'typical', and that this is to be contrasted with the analogue 'copy'. Firstly, this variability of digital images makes it difficult to determine the context of their production and therefore understand or indeed control their subsequent interpretations. Secondly, variability allows for the unprecedented mobility of the digital image through potentially infinite contexts, *intensifying* the polysemic nature of image interpretation.

In the first case, then, the variable digital image – an image that can be diachronically and synchronically present in multiple formats – is not fixed in a material context which shapes its meaning. There is no original and copy, only *versions*. Where analogue copies were more or less identical, it is equally significant that their new uses were fairly easily documented. For example, in the domestic sphere, copies may have been produced from negatives and given as gifts to relatives or friends. They may then have been framed and displayed, or perhaps had their visual content annotated with a description on the back of the print. These practices contextualize the photo and frame its possible interpretations within a limited field of circulation; we can recognize this most clearly in its absence – when we try and understand an old family photo with no inscription, for example ('Does anyone know who this is?'). There are often material clues through which judgements about the content can be made – the faded paper, the care or lack of care given to the framing, the juxtaposition of the photo in an album series, and so on. By contrast, in theory, digital images can be infinitely multiplied, leaving no traces of their uses other than perhaps a date. They do not necessarily reside in an album, in a definitive hierarchy or order, and in the case of digitized analogue photos may not contain the discernible traces of their prior material context.

These views have been strongly expressed within professional archival communities, who are currently being encouraged to digitize their vast collections in order to make them 'more accessible'. From the archivists' point of view, it has been convincingly argued that the meaning of photographs as documents lies in the identifiable contexts of their use rather than just in their visual content or material form (see Schwartz 1995). The reproduction of analogue images has to be understood in terms of how and why such duplicates or copies are put to use. How and why are some images created, reproduced, stored, shared or discarded? The difference between analogue and digital images here is not so much the visual content but the inability to identify the dimensions of use that are not materially 'present'. For some, digitization is highly problematic in regard to this sense of meaning:

> This digital shadow obscured the carefully documented balance of power between materiality and context that is critical to the determination of photographic meaning. Equally the digitizing process translates what was once a complex multilayered laminated object into something much more ephemeral. Where once materiality and meaning were bound up in a complex, synergistic and symbiotic relationship, the resultant digital object is an ephemeral ghost whose materiality is at best intangible. (Sassoon 2004: 199)

The difficulties of identifying authorship and the context of meaning are exacerbated where digital photos are produced without reference to an external reality. The 'computerization of culture' (Manovich 2001: 19) stemming from the convergence of media and computing makes it difficult to discern human intent and authorship when algorithmic codes create and re-create digital images. Although the rhetorical notion of a purely human author is required to emphasize the significance of the non-human computer, the role of the algorithm in enabling and constraining the possibilities of variation is significant. This conception of the primacy of technical code tends to abstract (or ignore) the history and the present diversity of the photographic image from its uses, conflating practice with form (e.g., Poster 2006). As Kember (2003) observes in her critique of deterministic approaches to digitization, the ability to produce realistic digital images 'out of nothing' provokes different reactions from the digitization of existing photos. It is the idea that the 'object-world is not regarded as being simply mutable but totally malleable'

Figure 3.1   Photoshop manipulation

(2003: 205–6) that is especially significant, as the production of digital images without reference to an analogue counterpart has become far more pervasive at the present time, notably in advertising and digital games. It also prompts reflection on the issue of indexicality, where, rather than being made infinitely variable *through* digitization, there is no original referent. As Rosen puts it: 'the production of the digital begins with numbers as its mediating materiality, therefore it can do without an origin in a profilmic "here and now"' (2001: 306). The technical continuity of the analogical photograph is ruptured because of the introduction of variability *into* the process of image production. This, in turn, opens up the digital image to further algorithmic variations, as they become indexed and searchable in image databases such as Getty Images or Flickr (Taylor and Harris 2005).

Variation and flow

The variable or 'liquid' form of the digital photo enables its mobility through interconnected information systems. This involves its reassembly in multiple locations – on a web page, in a software program such as Photoshop or iPhoto, or within photo-sharing sites such as Flickr and Facebook. The single image may no longer be made meaningful by its location within a traditional album, but instead is placed in multiple and shifting series of other images. In their work on the 'networked image', Rubenstein and Sluis argue that the significance of the stream now outweighs that of the single image. The multiple ways in which images can be organized and reorganized in different sequences is quite different to the linear narrative of the album:

> Within this flow of images the value of a single photograph is being diminished and replaced by the notion of a stream of data in which both images and their significances are in a state of flux. Disassociated from its origins, identified only by semantic tags and placed in a pool with other images that share similar metadata, the snapshot's resonance is dependent on the interface which mediates our encounter with it. (Rubenstein and Sluis 2008: 22)

But, in contrast to the notion that digital images are immaterial, the digitization of images enables their conversion into multiple material forms, from the continued use of printed album formats, 'digital frames', web-based repositories, hard drives, and so on. What is new about this? A distinction can be drawn between the ways in which mechanically produced photographs were reproducible and distributable as 'copies' in mass production and how digital images are both reproducible and variable in mass customization. The informational character of the digital image changes how it can circulate, who can access it and, given the number of contexts within which it can be embedded, what it can mean. This involves several rather different forms of reproduction and variation, including the vast image banks of stock photography documented by Frosh (2003) and the increasing numbers of ordinary images distributed through photo-sharing websites (Van House 2007), which also may act in turn as repositories for the stock photography industry. Although some have argued that digital snapshots are not meant to be archived (van Dijck 2007; Van House et al. 2005), it does not mean this will not occur. As will be shown in chapter 5, snapshots may be archived as a matter of unintentional routine with unforeseen consequences. The impossibility of controlling the flow of images, in terms of their meaning or their location, figures in debates about authenticity but also raises important issues about intellectual property and cultural production.

From the discussion above, it is clear that the process of digitization alters the material character of the photograph, allowing single images to become more 'liquid' in form. This enables them to be created and re-created outside of the original/copy relationship of reproduction established in the late nineteenth century. It also opens them up to the flows of information in computer networks (Lash 2002), which makes images simultaneously more accessible and subject to reinterpretation within vast streams of images. The new materiality of the photograph multiplies the possible 'lives' that it may have *simultaneously*, from existing in online databases, to becoming valued visual content, to being printed and stuck on the refrigerator.

Manipulation and authenticity

The versatility and malleability of the digital image discussed above leads to the question of whether digital images are always manipulated. The most influential argument about the increased distance between digital images and reality has been that they are so *easily* manipulated (see, for example, Manovich 2001; Mitchell 1992; Winston 1995). During the 1980s and 1990s, digital photography was discussed almost entirely in terms of manipulation and the collapse of the positivism, realism or indexical authenticity of the photograph, examined in chapter 2 (see Robins 1995). While this is a well-worn debate within the specific domain of photography studies, there are several aspects that have a bearing on changes in digital photography between the late 1980s and the present. While earlier debates about manipulation referred mostly to the digitization of analogue images via scanning and their sub-sequent manipulation on a PC, the production of malleable digital images from scratch is now the norm. Moreover, the shift from the relatively isolated instances of digital manipu-lation (in professional photography) to the current ubiquity of malleable digital images in everyday life is significant for rethinking some of these debates. In what follows, I will out-line some of the different ways in which digital manipulation has been understood and practised.

Cultures of manipulation
It has been argued that the malleability of digital images deconstructs the modernist fiction that photographic images authentically document reality (Mitchell 1992). Mitchell saw the burgeoning use of computing in image-making during the late 1980s as producing a radical break with the positivist visual culture of modernity, arguing that 'a worldwide net-work of digital imaging systems is swiftly, silently constituting itself as the decentred subject's reconfigured eye' (1992: 85). Developed in association with a poststructuralist critique of modern visual culture, Mitchell and others argued that digiti-zation takes us into a 'post-photographic era':

> The digital era, the current third photography, ongoing since the middle 1980s, surrenders and substitutes unconfuted factualness for easy fabrication. Given digital photography's nearly undetectable ability to gerrymander truth, words are needed to outline and anchor what might be untrue to the eye. The intangible digital reality refutes, even denies, our historical, scientific understanding of photography. Photographers have entered new territory and have become optical painters with light. (Cohen 2007: 220)

Digital images embody some of the characteristics of post-modernity in the same way that the analogue photograph mirrored aspects of modernity. For Mitchell, the false

Cartesian centredness of photography – the Olympian vantage point of the individual photographer and lens – has been replaced by the decentred 'electrobricolage' of fragmented digital images – without discernible origin or author. Digitization de-couples positivist notions of visual truth and authenticity (established through the dominance of perspective, focus, and so on) from photographic images. A major implication of this is the removal of an epistemological and ethical ground for authentic photojournalism or any form of evidence, which then becomes a matter of individual or institutional integrity and trust (Ritchin 1990) mirroring the shift from legislation to interpretation in postmodernity (Bauman 1990), in which a whole range of authoritative knowledge is questioned (such as medical, intellectual and scientific knowledge). The concern at the time was that, despite the knowledge that journalists had always routinely staged or altered documentary photographs, digitization takes such a common practice a stage further, increasing the ease and likely probabilities of manipulation (see Kember 1998). As van Dijck says, in relation to digitization and epistemological debates: 'Computers are bound to obliterate even the illusion of fixity: a collection of digital data is capable of being reworked to yield endless potentialities of a past' (2007: 47).

But in contrast to Mitchell and others arguing for the discontinuity of the digital image, some have maintained that, as there is nothing new about photographic manipulation per se, digitization simply *foregrounds* this as part of historically constituted processes of image-making (Rosler 1991). The argument can be made that the photographic image has *always* been manipulated – or indeed is by definition the product of manipulation – if we interpret the photograph as an outcome of the technologies, know-how, bodily dispositions and normative visual conventions that produced it. Photographs are not neutral in any sense, and it is a mistake to regard so-called straight photography as a historically dominant form rather than simply as one of many genres (Manovich [1995] 2003).

Photographs are necessarily partial documents of the real, through which elements are selected or excluded, made visible or invisible, and are often subject to staging of one kind or another. Even in the case of photographs used as legal evidence, they are routinely subject to claim and counter-claim and are, in this sense, constellations of material and discursive claims-making practices (rather than straightforwardly reliable documents of reality). In addition, the more self-conscious forms that image manipulation might take – such as the deliberate removal of aspects of the image, the cutting and pasting of multiple images, or the use of photography as a mode of self-transformation – have also been present from the nineteenth century (perhaps the most famous examples being Joseph Stalin's continual removal of figures from photographs once they had been executed).

In this sense, while pertaining to the actual business of engaging with digital images, the argument for radical discontinuity is developed from the technical characteristics of the digital image rather than from practices of digital photography. In some cases, the argument is strengthened by its juxtaposition with a simplified account of prior practice (Manovich [1995] 2003), or of producing 'elective affinities' with the broader critique of structuralist models of language (Lister 2000). The ascription of realism to the materiality of analogue images in the first instance is highly problematic. As Bolter and Grusin argue:

> The process of digitizing the light that comes through the lens is no more or less artificial than the chemical process of traditional photography. It is a purely cultural decision to claim that darkening the colour values of a digitized image by algorithm is an alteration of the truth of the image, whereas keeping an analogue negative longer in the developing bath is not. (1999: 110)

In this way the alteration of images becomes a problem only if one believed in the original transparency of photography and maintained a context-free theory of authenticity. The significant effect of debates about digital manipulation has not been to problematize the digital image quite so much, but to prompt a reflexive sensibility about the historical claims to documentary in the first place. This was partly Mitchell's point in emphasizing that the digital image, while privileging manipulation and indeterminacy, can usefully deconstruct modernist rhetorics of vision.

Nonetheless, whatever we think about manipulation, there are now radical possibilities for new combinations of visual data clearly evident in contemporary visual culture. Digitization allows for images to be constructed from arbitrary sets of data drawn from myriad sources, rather than primarily through the conjunction of body, camera and subject. Given the sheer range of available images, the extent to which they can be remade, and the number of sources from which they may be drawn, it seems clear that the centred perspective of the photographer is no longer the dominant perspective through which the world is 'seen'. For example, many of the images with which we engage in everyday life are composites of images and ideas drawn from a variety of sources, and in this sense they do not have an empirical referent.

The clearest and perhaps most pervasive example of this is in advertisements, in which the ability to produce 'born digital' images is celebrated (Frosh 2003). Flicking through any popular magazine, one is faced with image after image of commodities that are either computer generated or enhanced, and inserted within other images generated elsewhere. For example, a commodity (such as a car) may be a computer-generated image rather than an actual car, inserted within a landscape that is itself a composite of sky, trees and road cut from other images, and so on, the result of which might still be 'photo-realistic'. The point here is that digitization is often used to produce simulations of the photographic even though no external object has been photographed as such. The acceptance of such simulations – the representation of a reality that doesn't exist – pervades advertising and, if we include moving images, also computer games and contemporary cinema. In the case of personal photography, iPhone photo-sharing applications such as Instagram enable users to recontextualize images using a range of filters that simulate photographs made with the iconic Polaroid and Kodak Instamatic cameras. While these images have an empirical referent, the simulation of specific moments in photographic history is another way in which, as van Dijck (2005) argues, the *modified* public image has become culturally acceptable. Such a shift towards the normalization of manipulation has been discussed recently in relation to broadly political images and to the current pervasiveness of *photoshopping*. This is about the means of manipulation made easily available through the digitization of the image, and it is worth thinking about two examples here.

In the first case, models for Ralph Lauren had images of their bodies 'enhanced' through Photoshop manipulation in such a way that they appeared dramatically thin. We see here the continuation of a modernist 'gaze' objectifying the female body taken to an exaggerated extreme, the nature of which has prompted intense critique across the popular media (see www.psdisasters.com/2009/10/ralph-lauren-hits-keep-on-coming.html). On the one hand, there is a perpetuation of photographic objectification within the advertising industry. On the other hand, the routine nature of manipulation (it is simply *expected* that images such as these are airbrushed) is exposed when the models in question have ceased to look realistic in the sense of being 'realistically enhanced'. The shifting ground of what counts as 'authentic' seems to undermine any normative claims for the relationship between photograph and reality.

A second example further highlights an important question about the ubiquity of malleable images in contemporary culture: does the proliferation of malleable images promote a culture of routine deception or a heightened critical reflexivity about visual mediation and the *ambivalence* of authenticity?

In 2008 Sepah News – the media arm of Iran's

Revolutionary Guard – released an image of four missiles being fired to signal recent advancements within the field of nuclear weaponry to the international media community. While the image initially garnered international coverage and concern, occupying the front page of several large newspapers, including the *Los Angeles Times* and the *Chicago Tribune*, online photo enthusiasts quickly began declaring the image a manipulated fake (see Nizza and Lyons 2008). Several online photography communities, using their shared knowledge of photo-editing software, demonstrated how the image had been doctored; the original image had three missiles as opposed to four and also documented the presence of a military vehicle. According to further investigations led by the American Intelligence office, only one of the missile bodies had nuclear capability, which also challenged the original rhetoric surrounding the image (Scarlett 2010). There has since been a range of playful images depicting thousands of missiles, missiles falling from the sky like rain, and so on (see www.buzzfeed.com/scott/fake-iranian-missile-photos).

In the Iranian missile case it seems that the increased presence and circulation of digital images on the Web makes them subject to heightened critical reflexivity. What is also interesting in both cases is the nature of the *claims* for authenticity brought to bear on such images – claims for photo-realism continually surface in relation to what is presumably an 'unacceptable' level of modification. The insertion of the digital image into the broader networks of digital culture means that people are increasingly aware of its malleability, and as such there are *cultures of manipulation* that have a degree of cultural legitimacy and authenticity and others that do not.

Practices of authentic manipulation
Within the domain of personal photography, Rubenstein and Sluis (2008) suggest that prominent arguments about manipulation during the 1990s have been effaced by the current ubiquity of photography. Similarly, Susan Murray (2008)

makes a strong case for bracketing the issue of manipulation, especially when it is tied to a 'before and after' story of digitization, because amateur photographers rarely consider the truth value of their photos in practice. Authenticity cannot simply be transposed from technical conditions. The transformation of the camera (its insertion into other devices) and the palpable significance of the 'realist' digital snapshot in, for example, contemporary journalism and web-based photo-sharing seem to attest to this. Indeed, as Gunthert (2008) has argued, it is precisely the accepted realism of the Abu Ghraib images that places digital imaging *within* the history of photography rather than as a break from it. However, in drawing upon interviews with amateur photographers, I will argue here that there has been a *broadening* of the ways in which manipulation is defined, practised and interpreted in personal photography that is worth considering in more detail. This can be usefully explored in terms of identifying the 'authentic intent' of manipulation rather than whether the process is deemed significant or not. For example, as Frosh (2003) observes, the ethical crisis in photojournalism has not been replicated elsewhere, whereas in advertising digitization is positively valued as enabling different practical possibilities for reconfiguring images. This relates to the point made in chapter 2 that advertising now serves as the model for photography. Similarly, when we look at personal photography, it is becoming apparent that manipulation is understood and practised, if at all, in a variety of ways in relation to different communities or contexts of authenticity.

For example, we should ask whether the manipulated news photograph is different from a 'playful' snapshot of a family member or an 'enhanced' image to be entered in a photography competition. In some cases, such forms of manipulation are valued as skilful and as craft. There are emerging repertoires of digital photographic practice that incorporate some of the new possibilities and, although they reconfigure practice to some degree, are often subsumed into an earlier discourse of human-centred creativity associated with art photography. It would seem crucial, then, given the variety of meanings that 'manipulation' can have and the ways in which it has been practised historically (from staging the subject to post-production alteration), that the issue is approached empirically at the level of practice among those engaged in digital photography.

In what follows I will simply show how there are several aspects to the ways in which people articulate manipulation. Firstly, it is rarely referred to as *manipulation*. Many more nuanced accounts of practices of alteration are evident, which are significant in situating manipulation within contexts of everyday performance rather than as abstract possibilities. Secondly, there is a routine or habitual nature to some of these practices that confirms the notion that digitization makes manipulation unavoidable or at least implied. Alternatively, there is little sense that such practices have any relation to notions of deceit, fabrication or a lack of realism. In many ways they seem to reproduce the conventions of photo-realism, as it has been understood in everyday life rather than in theory. One of the most mundane forms that manipulation takes is the 'shrinking' of images, most commonly so that they can be sent via email. When sending photos, people routinely alter the colour saturation and cut and crop to frame:

> Yeah, sometimes I shrink images to send them through email so they're not so huge. I've sold a few things online, so I've, you know, cut out the cat on the side so . . . you know just cut and pasted a little bit. Umm . . . we took pictures of the buskers' festival at night and they were pretty dark, so we sort of lightened them a bit. They're not particularly good quality, but you can see what's happening now. We kept them where we could have ripped them previously. I experiment a little bit with sharpening images and colouration, sort of saturation and black and white images a little bit. (S, stage manager)

Such practices are rarely considered in terms of truth or deceit but as a pragmatic way of producing an authentic account of what people wish to convey. In this sense the communicative possibilities of the image are being shaped by the technical architecture of digital networks. The difference between technical capacity and actual practice is articulated within the most mundane activities of everyday life, where the constraints of time prevent people from utilizing camera or software features:

> I rotate them. I might zoom in on something. A few pictures I've tried to . . . you can lighten it up or darken it if the pictures aren't really showing it. It is kind of cool how you can make changes. I think it does a lot more than I do with it. And I know when I first started with the digital, this friend of mine, she tried to show me all the capabilities of it, and she said 'You know, you can do this, and you can . . . you know, if your bra strap is showing you can move skin tones over there so it's covered.' And I started to think that's just . . . there's no way I can start mucking about with my pictures to make everyone . . . I can barely get the film ones in an album, let alone if I start making every picture perfect. So I don't do a whole lot of touching up. (M, administrator)

If we switch to the context of the more 'serious amateur', then such practices are frowned upon or at least require rhetorical justification. Clear lines are drawn between the 'manufacture' and the 'enhancement' of photos. The digitization of photography has been accepted within amateur photographic societies and clubs, but this has been far from easy. New aesthetic and technical criteria have been invented, specifying which new technical possibilities are admissible and which are not. The negotiation between strong accounts of visual authenticity ('you just capture what you see'), the embracing of new technologies, and the maintenance of the photographer's skill level produces an ethics of amateur photography that privileges the realist image by bracketing its new conditions of production:

> That's the big thing. And that's come up in the photo club, the photo club which I'm a member of. And what people

don't seem to really want to . . . they don't get as worked up over it as I do. I really think it's a big concern. I think it's a big problem. That's the only drawback I feel. With everything else it's terrific. It's convenient, it's wonderful, and the ability to touch up or correct things in Photoshop is wonderful. I don't use Photoshop to manufacture pictures. That's not my interest. I want to capture . . . I'm old fashioned that way – I like to capture what I see. But, if something's dark and this and that, like I took a picture of my two neighbours, husband and wife, and I got a picture of them in their kayaks, turned out beautiful. But in the background there's this sort of landscape and hills in the background, and you can see these shacks, you know. So I thought they were distractions and in Photoshop I got rid of them. And it's all just the green background and the shacks are gone. (X, retired)

There are other practices of 'authentic manipulation' occurring, as amateurs become wedding photographers, citizen-journalists, and so forth (see chapter 4). For example, in the case below, the viewing pleasure of the image takes precedence both in private production and in producing the 'best' account of a wedding:

I've been to England a number of times. I get kind of tired of the sky in England being grey, right? So I called my friends in England. I said, 'Here's a scoop.' All my pictures of England now have the sky of Canada in them. Cause I'm sick of looking at the white sky, so I put the blue sky of Canada in my white sky of England. I have really nice England skies now, so . . . but I don't print those either. I'm just playing around, right? So, but I could take, you, the picture with the eyes closed, I've done this before with wedding photos that, you know, three of them have their eyes closed. I'll just chop and just do the bride and groom. Or that kind of thing. So I keep them. I just don't want people to see them because they'll think that that's my picture. but that's not the picture that I'm going to keep. (T, secretary)

While there are potentially endless variations in the precise ways that people conceptualize and practice manipulation, it is important to distinguish here between the notion that digital manipulation arises because of the *capacity* of the technology rather than its *application*. That the technology is habitually used to manipulate images indicates a prevailing *cultural normality*.

The materiality of digital code and the software within which it is often located enable an unprecedented number of possibilities to manipulate the image. There are also ways in which this is routine and unnoticed. But there are other ways in which it is a self-conscious act of 'enhancement'. The mutual constitution of technical and cultural elements arises through varied practices of digital photography. The technical ability to manipulate becomes instantiated in some practices and not others, but the number of moments at which manipulation *could* be practised has increased. In this sense the digitization of photography lends itself to the heightened self-reflection that characterizes late modern culture (Bauman 2000; Giddens 1994; Featherstone 2007). We often think that our personal photographs serve to remind us of 'what happened' in the past, what we used to look like, and perhaps what we 'felt like' in those specific moments (most likely birthdays, etc.). But looking at these images involves the construction of the past as much as its recall. Images that we have of ourselves are often reworked in relation to the present and as positioned towards an anticipated future (see van Dijck 2007). The issue here for van Dijck is not that digitization *causes* greater levels of manipulation – in this case for retouching one's past, potentially multiple times – but rather that aspects of digital photography enable increasing points at which one can engage in selective negotiation with the image. For example, the possibility exists at the moment of image capture and storage via the viewfinder, and later through computer software, plus later still with the latest printing technologies. Moreover, it is possible to copy the digital image infinitely and produce multiple versions of the 'same' image. They become 'living pictures' in that sense (ibid.: 106).

Throughout the discussions above, the relative importance of technology and culture is central to identifying the continuous and discontinuous elements of photographic manipulation. For example, as van Dijck points out, it is still not clear whether this 'condition of modifiability' arises primarily through the technology or through a culture which seems to *value* such modifiability, especially in terms of self-identity and consumption (see Bauman 2007). This might be usefully counterposed to the increasing use of 'straight' photographs in institutional practices of identification and social inscription (passports, ID cards, criminal records, etc.) As is evident above, identifying the possibilities inscribed in the collection of technologies is quite different from claiming that this translates easily into the realms of actual practice. It is equally plausible that people maintain the conventions of personal film photography through their use of the digital – that they fully embrace these moments of modifiability in an explicit sense. It must be remembered that, while theories of photography have questioned the photograph as document, in various ways it has been treated largely as 'realistic' at the level of everyday life. The extent to which the documentary authenticity of the digital image is seen to matter is crucially dependent on its socialeconomic, cultural and political context.

For example, there seems to be a difference between the significance attributed to images of the medical body in terms of how and whether they may be treated as authentic and those of, say, contemporary photographic art. Clearly, the consequences differ markedly: belief in the authenticity of the brain scan is not the same as belief as to whether an image can be considered 'art' or not. In more ambivalent territory, some digital war reportage is subject to great critical scrutiny in terms of manipulation (such as degrees of building damage), whereas some has become iconic precisely because of the attribution of authenticity (such as images of the degradation of prisoners). Of particular interest is how any limits to the extent of manipulation are established and how these might differ across different communities of practice. Some of these limits might be legislative and regulatory in terms of professional practice, for example in journalism. They may also emerge in an ad hoc manner through discursive means and consensual agreement, for example in an amateur photographic society that has conventions for what is considered manipulation. The acceptable limits of manipulation may take a more subtle form among personal photographers, where existing cultural norms concerning the representation of others, in the case of nudity or inappropriate behaviour, have remained continuous from film to digital.

The point here is that the arguments about digital manipulation have tended to be rather blunt instruments, unable to cast light on the potential subtleties of emerging practice. We should be cautious not simply to attribute authenticity and manipulation to film and digital respectively, as if these were straightforward characteristics of either the technologies or cultural practices. As suggested, one of the crucial recent debates about the digital image is that it has often been contrasted with the supposed realist and representational form of the film image, as if this were instantiated by technical means alone (Lister 2007). A great deal has been assumed about the role and interpretation of the film image in everyday practice, to which the digital is held against in far too stark a contrast. As we shall see in chapter 4, when the evolution of the camera is discussed, manipulation should be conceptualized as a social practice that co-evolves with the camera rather than as a technical capacity or normative humanistic concern. What we are seeing now is an increasing 'building in' of specific forms of manipulation to the materiality of practices in terms of the 'scripts' promoted by cameras and default software programs, for example in iPhoto software.

Ephemerality and durability

The word snapshot is the most ambiguous, controversial word in photography since the word art. It has been bandied

about as both praise and condemnation. It has been discussed as both process and product. A snapshot may imply
the hurried, passing glimpse or the treasured keepsake; its
purpose may be casual observation or deliberate preservation. The snapshot may look forward in time to a chaotic,
radically photographic structure, the appropriate equivalent
of modern experience; or it may look backward to the formal
portrait of a bygone age. (Jonathan Green in Hirsch 2000:
412)

The trope of authenticity has been discussed so far in relation to variation and manipulation. There are other aspects to
notions of authenticity concerned more with changes in the
aesthetics of photography after digitization. Digital images
may be ubiquitous, and their malleability may be taken to be
culturally acceptable at some level, but does ubiquity change
their cultural value in other ways? One often cited benefit of
digital photography among both manufacturers and practitioners is the simultaneous immediacy and disposability of
images, in that hundreds of images can be taken at no cost to
the photographer. Risks can be taken, skills can be enhanced,
thousands of images can be stored, and the perfect shot can be
obtained through continual 'snapping'. Even children can be
trusted to make their own images without wasting entire rolls
of film (see Shove et al. 2007). But does this also suggest a
downgrading of the cultural significance of *particular* images?
Can individual photographs be valued under conditions of
immediacy and ubiquity? As we saw in chapter 2, for some
commentators we are effectively drowning in ubiquitous
images, when theorized from the intellectual vantage point of
critical theories of commodification (Taylor and Harris 2005).
Following Sontag's (1979) critique of the 'superficial democracy' of the photographic image, Taylor and Harris assert
that mechanically reproduced photography leads viewers to
an uncritical acceptance of the world as mediated through
the photographic. The increased quantity of images at the
present time builds upon the industrialization of vision but

through digitization takes us into the realm of Baudrillard's (1981) 'fractal'. For these scholars, the ubiquity of digital photographs eradicates any sense of authenticity or originality in a condition of generalized simulation in line with the experience of postmodernity. Within the discipline of photography, this has been discussed in terms of the indexical depth of the analogue versus the depthless simulation of the digital. For example, in accounts of the loss of authenticity attached to the analogue, the realness of film in its grainy and material texture is juxtaposed with the 'cold perfectionism' of the digital image that exists only on screens. More recently, Lister (2007) and Murray (2008) have argued, following Manovich (2001), that making digital images actually involves data degradation rather than perfection. The imperfect or 'grainy' digital image has become valued as remediating the authenticity of the analogue (Lister 2007) and as a culturally valued or fetishized form in its own right (Murray 2008). Further to this, the overproduction of digital images and an awareness of routine alteration might create a more critical audience, while at the same time changing the consensus of appropriate or acceptable aesthetic values (Bate 2009).

In this latter regard, Murray (2008) argues that the sheer ordinariness, number and context-free nature of networked digital images make them unsuitable for the kind of textual analysis favoured by scholars of photography and critical theory. For Murray, looking from the ground up reveals new genres of the mundane emerging which signal a shift in image-making from the dominance of rarefied moments to the prioritization of everyday images in narrative construction. In analysing the content of images on the website Flickr, she argues that:

> the content of some of the most popular pages has little relation to traditional snapshot photography and is, in many ways, the opposite of pictorialist amateur photography (with its focus on realism, urbanization, and the small objects in life that often go unnoticed). It has little to do with studio

photography. It seems to speak to a new aesthetic and function – one dedicated to the exploration of the urban eye and its relation to decay, alienation, kitsch, and its ability to locate beauty in the mundane. Some have claimed that it is indeed a new category of photography, called 'ephemera'. (2008: 155)

This phenomenon has grown considerably even since Murray's observations. There are vast streams of images and discussions, particularly on Flickr, that explicitly concern the mundane or are tagged under the rubric of the 'ugly', and so on. In addition, the institutional effort to seek public knowledge and comment on thousands of ordinary images grows apace, from national archives efforts to collectivize memory to the US Library of Congress project of 'The Commons' (Scarlett 2010), to the routine use of ordinary photos in news journalism.

At the level of the individual, in a similar way to van Dijck (2007), Murray goes on to tie the prioritization of the everyday to changes in how life narratives are constructed in this public sense. Digital photos are seen as temporary, in line with the unfixed nature of late modern subjectivity, and made explicit in the ever changing online profiles of photo-sharers. In other words, any sense of disposability or temporariness arises not from the technology alone but is an outcome of novel practices of photo-sharing, which privilege continual 'updates'. This raises an important question about whether digital photos are *valued* in different ways from analogue as a result of technological change. The apparent indeterminacy and openness of the digital image would seem to promote ephemerality over durability. The idea of fixity and, to some extent, singularity brings with it a sense of durability. This might be thought of in terms of the temporality of material decay – of chemicals on paper, for example – or it might be used to describe historical longevity, or perhaps more commonly it implies a specific cultural value of things lasting or 'standing the test of time'. The association between printed photographs and durability

Figure 3.2   Capturing the mundane

or immutability is also bound up with a modernist conception of archival reason and temporality, and, less abstractly, with prevailing notions during the twentieth century of authentic personal memory ('I would save my photos in a house fire'). The large numbers of mundane digital photos produced in personal photography seem to be positioned as necessarily ephemeral and fleeting, perhaps as glances rather than considered reflections.

Ubiquity and mundanity

In several ways the ubiquity of mundane images raises questions of cultural value and authenticity. There is certainly a sense at the present time that we live in an age of visual publicization: that everything, however banal, is made into visual content. The notion of life becoming photographic was a long-standing concern during the twentieth century: 'Everything not photographed is lost, as if it never existed, and therefore in order to really live you must photograph as much as you can, you must either live in the most photographable way possible or else consider photographable every moment of your life' (Calvino, cited in Taylor and Harris 2005: 90).

It is well known that people make and keep and also share far more digital images than was ever the case with film images. How do people perceive these in terms of their value? If every aspect of everyday life has been made visual, then what kind of value can an individual's photos have? Drawing upon interviews conducted with undergraduates, I will show here how ubiquity problematizes modern notions of originality and authorship, but that people are finding other ways to make their photos feel like *their own*. A key point of interest brought up by respondents was using originality as a form of ownership. With so many cameras at a single event, many of the pictures posted on social networking sites like Facebook were seen as redundant. This quest to 'be original' in the face of such ubiquity was also seen in all of the respondents' personal photographs. Trying to find new ways of seeing was another way to 'own an image'. As H explained, everyone could now have a photograph of himself or herself at the Great Wall in China. In that way, neither the photograph nor the experience could be thought of as truly unique:

> I didn't print a photo of me on the Great Wall because I
> wanted to be a little more unique and not so distinctive where
> I was . . . Like, myself, I just don't want it to be that obvious
> and that everyone can relate to it. You know, I kind of want to
> keep the individualism behind it, (H, student)

She added that she finds her music (on her iPod) 'more personalized' now than her photographs. She said, 'I feel like everyone sort of has the same photos.' It does not matter who took the picture so long as someone took one. The lack of importance over who took the picture lessens the ability to claim it, or own the photograph and delimit or control its affective meaning. Again, it was only by photographing something in a unique way or capturing an original or personal subject that people could feel those photographs 'belonged' to them, almost regardless of what happened to them subsequently. In some ways the absence of an author was also an absence of responsibility for the content of the images posted up on sites like Facebook.

> You mean like everyday photos, like party photos, you and
> your group of friends smiling for the camera? I don't take
> them, but I would say that whenever, or when someone has
> a point and shoot and they put it in my face, my immediate
> reaction is to grab the person next to me and smile and put
> on this huge grin. (A, student)

The content of relatively conventional photo streams in Flickr or in Facebook reveals that, while many images reproduce the aesthetic conventions of twentieth-century albums – familiar poses, subjects and situations such as the wedding album – they routinely include what would have previously been called 'bad photography' – the banal or in-between moments not normally included in edited and ordered visual narratives. In some ways the rise of the mundane or throwaway image represents both the ability of digital cameras routinely to make thousands of images and the efforts on the part of practitioners to manufacture authenticity through this mundanity.

The precise negotiations between ubiquity, mundanity and authenticity enacted on the ground are of considerable importance in establishing this 'new aesthetics' of the everyday.

An important question here is the extent to which the (anticipated) sharing and ubiquity of images produces feelings of 'why take any pictures at all?', when it appears increasingly difficult to make them stand out from others. The sheer number of shared images, but also in the way they are ordered online, brings about this potential lack of specificity: 'Through the semantic mechanisms of tagging and metadata, the specificity of each online snapshot is obliterated by the way in which a single hyperlinked keyword can group together thousands of disparate images. Can 4,150,058 photographs tagged with "party" be wrong?' (Rubenstein and Sluis 2008: 24).

Another consideration is that individuals may have less choice about which images are valued and preserved as they are shared via information networks. The most mundane of images may have an extended online existence regardless of the wishes of the subject or author of the image. As will be explored in chapter 5, software 'animates' photos as they become penetrated with information, making them searchable and subject to continual recategorization and movement.

Concluding remarks

This chapter set out to explore the significance of ubiquitous photography at the level of the digital image itself. Of course, as will have been apparent, there is no 'image in itself' as such. Images are but one element of the configuration of technologies and practices that constitute photography, and this has always been so. But many of the arguments and debates about digital photography have centred on the image and need to be taken seriously on their own terms. It is evident that, over the last ten years in particular, the grounds on which these debates are conducted have shifted considerably. I have treated variability, manipulation and ephemerality as technical and discursive accounts of different materialities that have become *intensified* as digitization multiplies the possible trajectories that image-making can take. The shifts from analogue photographs to encoded digital images have been accompanied by divergent conceptions of the epistemology and ontology of the image. I have explained how the simple ascription of the real or the authentic to the analogue image has positioned the digital image as inauthentic in several ways, but that this is not an easy fit. The most common formulation has been that the malleability – the coded variability or the manipulation – of the digital image has rendered it either immaterial or context free, suggesting a radical break in the history of the photographic image and its meanings. I suggested that, in contrast to this, the question is now whether the cultural acceptability of the malleable digital image has prompted a reflexive sensibility about the nature of image-making, in terms of both practices of manipulation and the durability and specificity of particular images. It is of course worth reiterating that, at the level of ordinary practice, the majority of digital images are taken to be photo-realistic, reproducing many of the historical conventions of the genre. But I also showed how such a sensibility is evident in the ways people talk about both manipulation and ephemerality. We can begin to see potential diversity in the contexts within which manipulation is defined and actually takes place, each of which may have different implications and consequences. In focusing upon personal photography, the degree to which digital images are manipulated depends on what exactly is meant by manipulation, how this might be different from, say, enhancement, and what the expectations for image production and sharing are in a local context of visual communication. In other words, at the level of diversifying practices, we may find that the technical capacities of digitization – the possibilities afforded by the materials – are enacted differently in relation to established conventions and future aspirations among different constituencies. While for some scholars the issue of manipulation has become mute, partly through new forms of image valorization in the camera-phone (see Rubenstein and Sluis 2008), it remains important precisely because of the diverse ways in which it is understood.

While it is not entirely novel to argue that the digital image is very much a material image, this links to an important current argument across new or emergent media studies that considers the diversity of ways in which digital things can be *made material*. The fact that there is some debate over the technical characteristics of the digital image in the first instance raises important questions about the nature of theorizing at the intersection of media studies, sociology, and science and technology studies. More broadly, the emerging configurations of information (particularly software) and material forms (such as hand-held communication devices) presents us with another means of empirically examining the different and complex relationships between digital images and the material environments within which they are actually enacted and distributed.

CHAPTER FOUR

Technologies and Techniques: Reconfiguring Camera, Photographer and Image

Introduction

In the previous chapter I argued that the cultural significance of the malleable digital image lies in the diversification of material forms it can take in practice rather than in its disruption of the supposed representational qualities of the analogue photograph. While important, a focus upon the photographic image in isolation has clear limitations (see also Buse 2010). It has led to an overstatement about the novelty of the digital image in terms of its *threat* to the real (see Cohen 2003; Kember 2003). This has commonly resulted from the examination of abstract qualities of digital information – seeing digital images as technically free from material context – rather than the devices and systems through which digital information is materialized. In this way I think it has both neglected how the image is actually woven into different material contexts of meaning and value and masked some of the more significant continuities and discontinuities between film and digital at the level of technologies and their uses. In this chapter, I show how it makes as much sense to think of ubiquitous photography in terms of the *pervasiveness of interconnected technical artefacts* – cameras, laptops, cellphones and smartphones – as it does to think only about the character of images. Accordingly, the chapter locates the digitization of photography within debates about technological change in contemporary culture, asking to what extent changes in the material technologies of image-making and storage, display and distribution have shaped the dominant expectations and current practices of digital photography.

Critical discussions about photographic images have often placed the technology in the background, and with good reason. In seeking to avoid the charge of technical determinism, outlined in chapter 2, the stress in such accounts is on how vision is historically and culturally shaped and how notions of manipulation and authenticity can never simply be the outcome of technical devices (Batchen 2002; Lister et al. 2009; Osborne 2010). This may be quite right, but, as Lister (2007) has observed, the avoidance of any form of technical determinism has laundered the possibility that technologies have *any* agency and that there may be important aspects to the ways in which different technologies enable and constrain particular ideals and practices. I have argued that photographies are best understood as practices – practices that are made possible by and weave together ideals, technologies and forms of know-how in the production, consumption and management of images. Technology and culture are inextricably related and, accordingly, changes in the technologies of image-making, including but not limited to the camera itself, have consequences not only for the images produced but for the *activities* of producing, storing, displaying and distributing them, as well as the cultural conventions that regulate these activities. In other words, what counts as photography may be changing as a result of how technologies, techniques and users are reconfigured and co-evolve (Akrich 1992; Hand 2008; Shove et al. 2007; Van House and Churchill 2008).

There are two broad aspects of this to highlight here. On the one hand, it is essential to look at how particular social and cultural values become associated with and inscribed within technologies, shaping the possibilities of photographic agency. For example, since the late nineteenth century the value of mobility or portability has long been attached to consumer-level cameras, but appears to have a particular salience within present 'mobile lives' (Elliott and Urry 2010). Identifying the dominant scripts through which digital cameras are narratively positioned in this way is important and provides a sense of what kinds of expectations about what photography is, and what a photographer can or should do, are developed in tandem with the technology (Akrich 1992). On the other hand, it is also necessary to look at how digital cameras and other technologies are used in practice across different domains of social life. For example, it is arguably the case that the vast adoption of digital cameras allows more people than ever before to 'make basic choices about representation' in modes of imaging previously confined to industry and professionals (Cobley and Haeffner 2009: 125). The empirical question remains as to whether, and in what ways, the technical scripts of mobility, immediacy, networking, sharing, and so on, go on to be enacted by camera users.

To begin I will briefly discuss the reciprocal relationships between technologies, expectations and skills which frame the remainder of the chapter. I suggest here that the history of photography provides a number of insights into the mutual constitution of camera, photographer and image. Picking up on the conceptualization of technology and practice outlined in chapter 2, there are three key aspects to be examined further. Firstly, I will consider the rise of the digital camera and how its features and uses have changed the relations between camera and image. Film photography was arguably dominated by developments in the technologies of the image, whereas emergent ideals of digital photography have been shaped primarily by changes in camera technology, and how images can be made and used as a result. Digital cameras have incorporated many conventions of photography that were previously expected to be learned, such as framing landscape, lighting, portrait, and night shots, for example. This raises the question of how changes in the hardware are related to who is able to do photography, what kinds of skills and knowledge are required, and how aesthetic conventions and expectations of specific (photographic) genres are maintained or disrupted as a result. The implications for how such functions have become technologically stabilized and culturally valued have been considerable, especially the promise of a radical democratization of image-making offered by digital cameras themselves rather than in the subsequent manipulation of algorithms and pixels.

Secondly, I will focus upon the relation between camera and user in terms of how the conventions of skill and expertise, rather than the photographic image per se, are being reconfigured. The digital camera has intensified some of the contested rules of photographic practice, especially how the distribution of skills between the photographer and the camera are perceived. When we think of the sheer ease of conducting digital photography, the trained body of the photographer in framing, capturing and developing photographic images seems to belong to a bygone age. The camera-enabled accumulation of experimental skills, the individualization of the photographic process, and the generation of digital forms of expertise form the context for examining how non-human and human agency are redistributed in technological culture (Latour 2005).

Thirdly, I will discuss how the insertion of the camera and its ongoing reconfiguration within broader 'suites of technology' has reshaped the trajectories of digital photographic practices extensively and rapidly. Devices are always elements within broader chains of technologies, but this is particularly explicit in digital photography, as increasing numbers of devices and systems are designed to fit together in a landscape of converging technologies and systems. The phenomenon of technological convergence will be discussed in relation to how digital cameras have become part of an ever shifting constellation of technologies, from laptops to memory sticks, and also *within* other devices such as cellphones, laptops, tablets and smartphones. The specific convergence of cameras with telecommunications has become the most important aspect of digital photography and perhaps digital culture more broadly, enabling a radical diversification of visual communication.

Technologies, expectations and skills

As discussed in chapter 3, the photographic image has been shaped by the technologies used to produce it, the conventions and expectations of what counts as a legitimate image, and the varied practices of photographers. New technologies emerge within existing frameworks of expectation and convention while also having the capacity to disrupt them (Shove 2003). Such a capacity can be seen clearly in the history of photography, where specific technical skills are required to be a competent photographer, distinguished from a 'mere amateur', and new technical forms threaten established ways of doing things. In principle, new technologies may radically extend the parameters of practice or all but reproduce existing practices. Despite this ambivalence, from the point of view of serious practitioners of the art, the medium of photography appears continually under threat from newer technologies, which, for the most part, promise *ease*. For example, a historical parallel can be drawn with digitization in the shift from wet-plate to dry-plate collodian photography in the late nineteenth century:

> [The wet-plate bore] is a person with a past, of which he is more or less justly proud, who looks upon the dry-plate man – who has merely to flow a colourless solution over a yellow film in order to produce a negative – as having come into some privileges which he had not earned by experience. Not one modern photographer in a thousand has the smallest sympathy for the wet-plate man . . . in photography, as in everything else, the fittest survives, and the fittest negative process is gelatino-bromide on glass, paper and film. (*Photographic News*, 20 April 1900)

Such a transition produced much consternation among wet-plate practitioners – about the *loss* of skill and knowledge, the creeping ignorance of the dry-plate users, and the relative ease with which *anyone* could produce photographic images. The convenience of the dry-plate collodian process and low-priced prints enabled the market for family portraits and images of public figures to expand. Indeed, it has been argued that such a sociotechnical reconfiguration of photographic practice is more significant than the 'invention' of photography itself, for it is only when photographs move beyond paintings in their mass circulation, and when their reference point becomes *photography* rather than painting, that a distinctive medium or new way of seeing emerges (Baylis 2008). Of course, this is inseparable from the insertion of photography within expanding telegraphic, commercial and transport networks, all of which altered the possibilities of both the visual content and the distribution of photographs. However, none of these technical changes become significant unless they are *practised*. In that sense, the co-evolution of technology, expectation and skill through practice lies at the crux of how photographies change, whether they are analogue or digital.

This theme of democratization, real or perceived, has been an important one in framing responses to new technologies and techniques, and this is no different in relation to photography. In addition to innovations in image processing and production, similar responses to changes in camera technology can be observed in the historical literature. Perhaps the most famous invention – the Kodak camera of 1888 – enabled a fundamental alteration of the relationships between photographer, camera and subject, by removing any requirement to know how the camera or chemical process worked and, most importantly, any ability to produce images without *training* (Latour 1991). As George Eastman described:

> Photography is thus brought within the reach of every human being who desires to preserve a record of what he sees. Such a photographic notebook is an enduring record of many things seen only once in a lifetime and enables the fortunate possessor to go back by the light of his own fireside

to scenes which would otherwise fade from memory and be lost. (Quoted in Hirsch 2000: 173)

Before this, during the nineteenth century, physical characteristics such as those of weight and bulk limited the spaces and situations in which cameras could be used, and long exposure times restricted the range of photographic subjects further still. Both the 'stereographic' camera and viewer and the 'carte de visite' or 'card photograph' camera became popular in conjunction with the collecting practices in the late Victorian era, by the end of which millions of images had been produced. From the mid-nineteenth century, photographic clubs and societies emerged, which traded images, published journals, promoted exhibitions and disseminated technical information (Marien 2006). Perhaps most importantly, these societies, such as the Photographic Society of London (1853), were in part responsible for the establishment of the criteria for photography and photographers. Early photography was almost exclusively a male pursuit, although many (wealthy) women participated in such clubs.

By the start of the twentieth century, cameras were mobile and were used to make new kinds of images in new contexts. They were commercially viable and relatively simple to operate. The Kodak Brownie became the first mass-marketed portable and affordable camera in 1900, with the first 35 mm still camera arriving in 1914. The expansion of personal photography developed apace from 1935, when the portable camera could be used with commercially viable colour films (Kodachrome). During the 1950s, personal photography became narratively positioned as a defining feature of normal domestic life, with several new technologies being associated with the making, viewing and display of photos in the home. In terms of technology, expectation and skill, removable film differentiates using the camera to make images and the actual development of those images, distinguishing the amateur photographer from the self-developing professional or 'serious amateur'. The Polaroid instant camera (1948), instant colour film (1963), one-step instant photography (1973) and the first point and shoot camera (1978) were subsequent technologies that further continued the process of embedding photographic processes within the camera itself. The apparent simplicity of the point and shoot camera enabled marketing campaigns aimed at segmenting the photographic market, promoting specialized genres of photography (the manual complexity of the serious amateur camera; the casual simplicity of the holiday snap camera) and suggesting that any competent family (especially women) should be documenting its history and vitality through the new everyday photography (West 2000).

Several important themes emerge here. Firstly, aside from the rhetorical positioning of the Kodak and other cameras as available to everyone, the idea of the camera as a notebook rather than, say, an exclusive, expensive and cumbersome piece of specialist equipment retains its significance for the ways in which many digital cameras have been perceived in relation to their film equivalents. Similar ideas about snapshots and everyday photography circulated during the 1990s in comparison to the more advanced film cameras that still dominated the serious market. At the present time it is precisely the fact that people take cameras everywhere, and that imaging technologies are embedded in other devices, that contributes to their constant presence and their use as recorders of everyday mundanities. The relations between mobility and ubiquity and the chance 'never to miss a moment' also remain dominant advertising strategies today, when memory has morphed into the process of 'sharing' (explored in chapter 5).

Secondly, the association between the mobility and simplicity of the Kodak and the ability to preserve memories has always been Eastman Kodak's central advertising line (now reconfigured as Kodak 'easy sharing'). The lightweight mobility of the Kodak (along with other hand-held cameras of the late nineteenth century) freed up the potential subjects of photography, resulting in the arrival of the snapshot (a picture taken 'without aim'). The Kodak also enabled the emergence of a retail market, with standardized products and services (development, photofinishing). As Hirsch (2000) also observes, the ease of taking a snapshot altered the perception of what was worth taking and whether a 'mistake' mattered so much. People took chances and made errors, many of which became incorporated into genres of both photography and other mediums such as painting. The 'unexpected' appeared more often, and it became more common to see unusual angles, cropped and unbalanced frames, blurred images, and so on, which arguably influenced the understanding of perception in the visual arts in the early twentieth century and became manifest through new art movements such as surrealism. The relevance here is the ways in which the banal or the mundane *challenged* the dominant discursive and material legitimacy of photography, especially in terms of skill and expertise. We see similar issues arising today among societies of serious amateurs who have 'gone digital', but are keen to distance themselves from the notion that *anyone* can do photography, exemplified by the vast range of images uploaded to Flickr.

Historically continuous issues of a *perceived* decline in technical skill and professionalism shaped early responses to digitization, particularly the phenomenon of increasing automation where, for example, the digital camera collapses the distance between taking and viewing. That said, digital photography has all but eradicated film in professional *and* amateur communities, raising questions about whether and how distinctions between the two have been maintained through digitization. For example, in the realm of personal photography, it has been argued that the cameraphone instantiates an unmediated form of photographic practice:

> The ability to take photographs without becoming a photographer is appealing not only because it makes photography less technological but also because with the absence of the

> camera the photographer does not become an observer but
> remains intimately connected to the subject of photography.
> (Rubenstein and Sluis 2008: 21)

The key point here is how the reconfiguration of the photographer–technology–image relationship (as the camera
disappears inside another device) removes the need to 'be
a photographer'. Such a view is in many ways not new, as
each major development in technology has been framed as
changing what photography is and what it means to be a photographer. But, until very recently, the distinctions between
the serious amateur and the popular photographer were maintained in terms of the promotion of specific technologies and,
by implication, skills towards particular markets through, for
example, photography magazines. In what follows, the technical shifts in digital camera technology will be discussed in
terms of the specific promises and threats they seem to produce and how such cameras are used.

The rise of the digital camera

The sociotechnical evolution of the camera has been fundamental in constituting the possibilities of photographic
practice, including the relative agency of technology and photographer. The general novelty of the digital camera in this
regard is the erasure of the time between making, viewing
and distributing pictures. As suggested in chapter 2, a focus
on the camera and its features does not necessarily entail a
technically deterministic perspective when these features
are understood in relation to the evolving cultural expectations and conventions that have shaped and are shaped by
them in practice (Lister et al. 2009). For example, when I
was interviewing early adopters of mass-marketed consumer-
level digital cameras in Paris in 2002, it was apparent that
some people saw the digital camera *as a camera*, while others
thought of it as something entirely different. The relationship

between the technical features of the device and its design resemblance to a film camera were ambivalent, depending on the ways in which cameras are actually used, in relation to other cameras, technologies and social situations. Some people replicate their film-based practices with digital cameras, where others engage in 'unphotographic' acts of imaging as a form of note-taking, while using a 'real' camera for established photographic acts, etc.

Different issues arise within other communities of practice. For example, the relationships between generations of reporters and editors in journalism have shaped the adoption and use of cameras, and digital cameras have enabled the 'mass deletion' of photos in the field, while the use of digital cameras in the legal system has co-evolved with new requirements for judging the authenticity of photographs as evidence (Meyer 2008). As such, this is not only a question of utility, or whether an individual considers themselves to be a photographer or not; it also involves the material possibilities enabled and constrained by cameras and other technologies which have been adopted in a massive consumer boom but are differentiated along several lines. There have been several trajectories in the development of the digital camera, each of which has been related to different expectations and uses. The design decisions made about digital cameras arose in relation to prior industry affiliation, with key differences in dominant technical features emerging in relation to photographic, electronics and computer industries (Benner and Tripsas 2010). That several trajectories are made possible by digital cameras at the levels of design, adoption and practice tells us something about the continued elasticity, ambivalence or 'interpretive flexibility' of the camera as a technical device (Bijker et al. 1987; and see Barry 2001).

A brief history
The emergence of digital photography as institutionalized, commercialized and ingrained in daily practice is inseparable

from antecedents in analogue photography, developments in computer science, governmental and militarized spying technologies (the Corona Project; NASA), and video imaging within the television industry during the 1950s and 1960s. The digital cameras recognizable today are the outcome of technical and cognitive convergence – specifically the use of the charge-coupled device and megapixel sensor within the body of the camera, and the development of peripheral devices for migrating images to other locations (CDs, memory sticks, PCs, modems, and so on). All of this has involved multi-sector developments in the photography, electronics and computing industries (Benner and Tripsas 2010), with the adoption and use of digital cameras occurring within particular institutional contexts, including government, private sector companies, scientific institutions, journalism, and so on.

Until the early 1970s, photographic images were fixed only by means of light-sensitive chemical reactions on the surface of a film or a plate. In 1969, Bell Laboratories developed a charge-coupled device (CCD) that converts light into voltage. Although it was many years before this process became widespread, the CCD is the key technology on which digital and television/video cameras depend and around which many forms of digital imaging now revolve, where the analogue image is converted into data (as described in chapter 3). Among prototypes of the contemporary digital camera were the first film-less electronic camera, patented in 1972 by Texas Instruments, and the Mavica electronic camera – described as 'the camera of tomorrow' – released in 1981 by Sony, which, while basically a television camera, was certainly seen within photojournalism as inaugurating the end of film (Dunleavy 2005). National Geographic photographer Emory Kristof was the first to use an electronic camera of this sort, for underwater images in 1979. Such cameras took video frames using CCD technology but did not themselves produce digital images.

These developments occurred before the advent of the digital camera as such, which arose through the convergence of

Figure 4.1   Camera evolution

several other elements, but has been similarly shaped through its proposed use in photojournalism, where the value of receiving images from around the world figured as the central *raison d'être*. In 1986 Kodak produced the first megapixel sensor that could record 1.4 million picture elements (megapixels) and from those produce a photo-quality digital print. Kodak also produced the Photo CD System in 1990 and the first commercially used digital camera in 1991 – the DCS (Digital Camera System), which was actually a Nikon F-3 camera with the Kodak megapixel sensor. The significance of this was that it converted analogue to digital *internally* – and in this sense can be thought of as a digital camera that is recognizably similar to those used at the present time. The use of the Nikon body stemmed from the routine employment of that model within photojournalism. The camera could then be connected to a Digital Storage Unit incorporating a hard disk (200 mb, 160 images) and a viewing screen allowing for immediate checking of the composition of the image. In 1992 this configuration was redesigned as one camera device, allowing for fifty images to be recorded internally, but it was in 1994 that the Digital News Camera (developed by Kodak and the Associated Press) appeared (at a cost of US$15,000) and importantly required no shoulder-mounted battery pack. By 1994 there were photojournalists using cellphones to transmit images from remote locations. This was partly to do with the Associated Press's high-speed digital photo transmission and receiver system, which – when coupled with the 'electronic mini-darkrooms' where photos could be converted into bytes of information – generated new expectations about how photojournalism might work in the future, especially in relation to submission deadlines (Dunleavy 2005).

Issues of picture quality and expense prohibited large-scale adoption of this camera, but it made concrete a set of new expectations about the relations between journalists and editors which has accelerated the rates of adoption since 1996, when 'digital photography . . . finally reached a stage where it is a deadline and production tool, rather than an expensive toy for computer-literate photographers' (Didlick, in Dunleavy 2005). These cameras themselves operate in a similar way to analogue cameras – they use lenses, apertures and shutters – but they convert light into digital information that is then compressed and stored on a mobile hard drive or memory card. After just a few years digital developed to the point at which it could compete with film photography across most applications. Increasing volumes enabled economies of scale, and the quickening pace of innovation had a huge impact on the industry, not only in camera manufacture but also in film and processing.

At the same time, designs with the ordinary consumer in mind were first available in the early 1990s, still with very low resolution and at a high cost. These domestic markets are absolutely central to the rise of ubiquitous photography. Picking up on my earlier point about consumer conceptions of the camera, Benner and Tripsas (2010) observed that different conceptions of the camera initially framed design decisions for consumer-level cameras. Photography firms such as Kodak positioned the digital camera as a point and shoot film camera (with optical zoom and high-resolution

Figure 4.2   Apple Quick Take, 1994

pictures), with printing a key capability. Consumer electronics companies such as Casio prioritized the video components (LCD displays, movie clip capabilities), seeing the digital camera as a camcorder of sorts. Cameras developed within the computer industry promoted these as PC peripherals, concentrating on the connections between PC and camera (with Intel calling their product a PC Camera in 1997). Computer firms also adopted the image manipulation components of zoom software to be utilized on the PC (Benner and Tripsas 2010). The technical and industry convergence around all of these dominant features can be seen in most consumer-level models at the present time, with most firms incorporating elements developed by previously rival companies.

In 1994 several models appeared that introduced different ways of moving images to other locations and technologies. For example, the Apple Quick Take 100, which stored eight images internally, could be connected to a computer via a serial cable. Olympus produced the Deltis VC-1100, which could connect to a modem and upload images to another camera or computer (this could take 6 minutes per image). From 1995 new photo reading and printing technologies were developed (Hewlett Packard, Epsom), alongside memory cards with ever increasing capacities, the ability to record sound alongside moving pictures (10 seconds at a time on the 1995 Ricoh RDC-1) and later, in 1997, the recording of moving images as MPEG files and still images as JPEG files (Hitachi MP-EG1, Sony Cybershot), as well as in-printer cameras (Fuji) that could print directly from the camera. The advent in 1999 of uploading images to the Web using PhotoHighway.com enabled photos to be transmitted directly from the camera and organized online, emailed, and so forth.

The coupling of the digital camera with previously unrelated hardware and software is the outcome of the privileging of this trajectory within the consumer electronics and computer industry sectors – both of which were growing exponentially – and specific industry collaborations, particularly between Kodak and Microsoft (Windows has the Picture Transfer Protocol as standard), such that Kodak's EasyShare range of cameras have always been compatible with Windows XP. The development of technical standards between cameras, cellphones, PCs, printers, and so on, has enabled levels of interoperability that have shaped what the digital camera is at least as much as the ongoing innovation in picture resolution and specific camera features. In this sense there has been design convergence around what constitutes 'a digital camera'. In the language of science and technology studies, these trajectories have scripted the possibilities of practice, making the mobility of digital images through interoperable technical systems the default expectation.

Indeed, to return here to the digital camera as computer peripheral, the advent of consumer-level digital photographic *practices* is related to the increasing use of computers during the 1990s in both the workplace and the home. For example, many digital cameras found their way into the home in the first instance not as replacements for film cameras but as something people were required to use at work (in surveying, real estate, architecture, law enforcement, and so on, interestingly enough as technologies of *evidence*) (see Lally 2002). Another route during the 1990s was where PC packages often came with a digital camera included as standard (the more recent equivalent being the 'gift' of a Blackberry to corporate employees), and presently most laptops, cellphones and smartphones have cameras embedded *within* them. This is not a teleological story of invention and need, of inevitability or progressive improvements with a rational outcome. Rather, much like the development of other technologies, it involves the simultaneous and often unrelated development of technical components with specific purposes in mind that become configured in other devices in the context of economic, social and cultural structures and practices (Misa 2004). In this sense, while consumers continue to acquire digital cameras as stand-alone devices, they also acquire them *haphazardly* as standardized elements within other technical systems related to different practices. This is one way that the daily production of images has become normalized and stabilized (Law 2004) and to some extent *routine* (Van House 2011).

At the simplest level, there are clear continuities and discontinuities between film and digital cameras. On the one hand, digital camera development diversifies from large-scale professional and specialist systems (in photojournalism and science) to consumer-level 'snapshot' cameras in a similar way to that of film cameras a century before. In this sense, the consumer-level digital camera represents the increasing blackboxing of image-making processes within a single device in the same way that film cameras did (Latour 1991). The speed at which innovation has occurred is dramatically faster, with components being developed and acquired across firms, and the specialization of cameras and segmentation of the market along photographic, electronics and computing lines being more widespread in the context of flexibility. On the other hand, while film cameras made the chemical process invisible, digital cameras have further incorporated into the device the processes of viewing, processing, manipulation, annotation, deletion and distribution. It is now arguably the case that the camera itself is becoming invisible as it evolves into a 'feature' of new digital devices. Moreover, the connection of the digital camera to a wide range of peripherals changes what kind of an object the camera is, and this may differ in relation to, say, journalistic and domestic uses. It has become both more significant than ever before, as a device in itself which incorporates previously human-orientated action, and less significant as it is transformed into one element within a dynamic ecosystem of devices and systems. It has been argued that, during the twentieth century, the main function of the camera was to sell film and processing techniques (Slater 1991). The digital equivalent would seem to be to make images distributable, both for commodification and for other forms of exchange, within digital information networks.

Promises and threats of the digital camera

An important component of the rise of the digital camera is how film and digital cameras were positioned in relation to each other over time. Electronic and digital cameras (rather than imaging) were developed for specific scientific and photojournalistic uses. But the intensive development of consumer-level cameras shifted the digital camera from alternative to replacement for film during the 1990s:

> The technology of the digital camera is being constructed as a replacement for analog/chemical technologies instead of an alternative technology with its own specificity . . . the 'remediation' of photography by digital photography is not to do with tendencies inherent in media, but to do with the process of finding new markets for innovations and with the cultural and ideological production of obsolescence. (Henning 2007: 53)

The popular narrative of digital camera development and adoption among ordinary consumers is one of increased ease of use, mobility, immediacy, picture quality and networked capabilities. But, as observed in chapter 2 in relation to consumption, developments within the photographic, electronics and computer industries do not simply translate easily into the construction of markets for products or actual consumer practices. The technical developments alluded to above have been narratively positioned in specific ways, in relation to industry and also to broader cultural values and ideals. Van House (2011: 132) has argued that the acceptance of digital technologies has been because digital photography did 'not significantly undermine the prior meanings of personal photography'. This is quite right for many people, especially those with less experience or previous connection to film. But, within the confines of professional and serious amateur discourse, the digital camera emerged during the 1980s and early 1990s as a distinct threat to some of the key components of photographic practice (for example, within the serious amateur magazine *Popular Photography*, which in June 1990 conceptualized digital as part of a 'crisis in photography') and to broader issues of digital visuality, memory and ubiquity (explored in chapter 5). At the same time, it was discussed in terms of its *promises* within computer-orientated discourse found in popular computing magazines such as *PC Photo* (June 1997), in which digital photography was initially 'computer photography', explicitly framing digital cameras as PC peripherals. Much of this reproduced the longer-term debate about *automation* in film photography, where decreasing levels of user manipulation at the level of the camera posed a threat to the autonomy of the photographer. Another way of thinking about this is how *agency* is distributed and redistributed between humans and machines (Latour 1999), in this case photographers and cameras in the production of images. I suggest here that digital cameras had to reproduce aspects of film photography while offering technical novelty in the configuration of several elements in order to become such a successful 'predatory' technology.

The notion of a 'decision-less camera' – with which most point and shoot digital cameras are identified – has a long history. As outlined earlier, the shift from dry- to wet-plate photography in the late nineteenth century was considered to offer easy access to previously honed skill. Such a dynamic can be observed continually throughout the history of the camera, with 'snapshot cameras' becoming the most popular among amateurs, particularly since the 1950s, and the more specialized semi-professional and professional cameras retaining some semblance of complexity at the same time. During the 1950s, *Popular Photography* routinely debated the issue of automation. In February 1958, the editorial claimed that 'automation is taking over life in general and also photography'. For the serious amateur, this represented a decline of the art, where 'we could end up back in Eastman's era', despite having 'worked hard for the stature of photography since that' (ibid.).

What is different about digital cameras in this respect? While embodying many aspects of the point and shoot, they have incorporated the post-production skills of the photographer – deletion, selection, modification, enhancement, and so on – into the image *production* processes with the 'touch of a button'. Within *Popular Photography* during the early 1990s, digital cameras were framed as likely to produce a 'decision-free photography' that was considered to offer freedom for the photographer, but at the cost of not understanding how cameras work. This in turn was seen as a threat to the ability of the photographer-camera to disseminate truths about the world (*Popular Photography*, April 1990). Since 2000, the digital camera has begun to be reframed as a camera where photographers have *more* control over the medium (as digital SLRs become increasingly affordable) in a way that fits with earlier cultural ideals of film photography. Indeed, up until the mid-1990s, film was being touted in *Popular Photography* as 'the original Photoshop', as 'not crashing', as 'not requiring infrastructure' and, most importantly, as 'not precluding digital' (June 1994). There was initially much disdain for digital point and shoots, which were 'simple instruments for the snapshooter interested in photographs rather than photography' (January 1995). It was not until 1996, for example, that competition winners in the magazine included computer-enhanced images. From 2001 the magazine split into film and digital sections, and in 2003 its name was changed to *Popular Photography and Imaging*.

A second key feature of the digital camera is the viewfinder – the screen on the back of the camera that shows what image the camera is initially 'seeing' and subsequently has made, and further allowing for a variety of editing processes to take place. The viewfinder is not new but has become a larger, multifunctional screen, changing how people hold and position the camera. We might also see the continuity here between the Polaroid camera and instant colour film (1963) and the digital camera. But this concept of photographic *immediacy* – the ability to see the image immediately after pressing the button – has been taken much further with the standardization of the viewfinder in digital cameras, because the image can not only be seen or printed but altered, deleted, annotated, shared or saved immediately afterwards. The Polaroid camera and film may have altered the subjects and situations of photography to some extent, but digital convergence shifts the temporal possibilities of decision-making *into* the production process. The possibilities for human agency in shaping the image seem to be multiplied here. It is equally significant that the viewfinder enables the *collective* viewing of images, regardless of whether they go on to be deleted, stored or distributed. In this way the viewfinder alters the possible uses of the camera as an object for viewing and communication, rather than only for producing photos.

The further materialization of the image-sharing process through information networks appears to differentiate the digital camera more substantially. While there is nothing new about the giving and receiving of photos, whether between friends or in professional contexts, the sociotechnical dimensions of how this occurs have dramatically altered since digitization. During the nineteenth century, a primary means of sharing portrait photos was through commercially manufactured *cartes postales*. Photographic studios would typically provide a series of props and bourgeois costumes for the production of images specifically to be shared with acquaintances and family. This practice of photo-sharing also became a wider commercial enterprise as collections of anonymous or celebrity portraits were developed, often of sexualized women. Interestingly enough, although this was a burgeoning and legitimate photo-sharing industry, the majority of images circulated as commercial commodities were of individuals who had neither intended their images to be disseminated in this fashion, nor consented to it. For example, on occasion images of 'attractive women' would not arrive at their final destination, as they were plucked out of the postal system and reproduced and framed as commercial goods (Scarlett 2010).

We can observe how digital cameras and their networked connectivity enable an intensification and diversification of these practices. As observed above, this has shifted from the connection of camera to PC via serial cable to the use of CDs, removable memory cards, and so on. Within *PC Photo* during the late 1990s and early 2000s, email figures as the most significant technology of sharing photos. At the present time, manufacturers such as Kodak have developed models that incorporate the sharing (distribution through information networks) capacity within the camera, linked to Wi-Fi networks. For example the Kodak EasyShare has materialized the process of sharing into the body of the camera with the 'share button', which enables photos to be uploaded automatically to photo-sharing platforms such as Flickr (Solomun 2011). This standardizes the practice of sharing, translating it into the device itself, producing a relatively open script for human action and one that, as examined in chapter 5, has become all but culturally unavoidable.

Another way in which digital cameras promise to standardize specific sociotechnical relations is the relation between image and place. From the nineteenth century the camera has

Figure 4.3   Geotagging camera

been bound up with conceptions and experiences of space and place in producing iconic representations and inviting further consumption of places through photography (Urry 2002). In fact, Benjamin (1999b) argued that the camera was uniquely suited to capturing and interpreting some of the bewildering transformations of urban experience during the early twentieth century. He was referring to what he called the 'optical unconscious', whereby the vision of the camera allowed for things previously unseen to be seen, and the speed and fragmentation of contemporary urban life to be coherently organized into a narrative form (such as film). This might also work *against* dominant representations of urban space, where the wandering figure of the *flâneur* can read and rework the spectacles of modern consumerism, by constructing an individualized narrative through photos. With digital cameras, the ordinary practice of making photos of place or landscape has also taken several new turns.

Existing practices of documenting and representing space and place are potentially extended with digital cameras, as they are carried more often, used to produce exponentially more images, document a far wider range of sites than in personal film photography (Lee 2009), and can be used for communicative visual practices during the act of image-making itself – most recently in conjunction with 'checking in' geolocational applications used in smartphones. In this latter sense in particular, the ways in which digital photos have become 'the new currency for social interaction' (van Dijck 2007: 62) promise a 'synergistic' relationship between photographer, place, image and others (Hardey 2007) through geolocational tagging. Lee (2009) shows how Sontag's (1977) observation that people walk in urban space as a 'strategy for accumulating photographs' has been radically extended to include all forms of movement, travel and social interaction. Several studies have shown how digital photos can be 'mashed up' with other representations of the city, especially within blogs and wikis which narrate the urban experience, whether individually or through commercial sites that promote specific places (see Hardey 2007). These new combinations of web-based image and text can then, in turn, become visual resources for new practices of urban mobility. Lee (2009) calls this the 'circuit of spatial imagery', showing how this, in a way, leads to an intensification of the 'tourist gaze' (Urry 2002), as individual photos circulate in web-based media, shaping people's anticipatory experiences of place, which they then explore with their digital cameras.

Further to this, the practice of writing the time and location on the back of film prints has been materialized in the digital camera, with the automatic dating of images and now the ability to locate them spatially with geotagging software such as Microsoft's Photosynth. Along with photo-sharing, digital cameras coming onto the market from 2009 onwards have increasingly incorporated geotagging capabilities. This spatialization of image-making, storage and distribution is a significant innovation in terms of the convergence of different corporations and their products, and also in cultural terms to do with how cameras mediate practices of travel and consumption outside of tourism.

Uses of digital cameras
In briefly examining the histories of digital cameras and the expectations they have generated, it becomes clear that many identifiable attributes – viewfinders, immediacy, and so on – have longer trajectories, embodying familiar promises in the context of new cultural and technological realities. The empirical question here is the extent to which material features of the digital camera alter how images are produced and managed. The specific stabilization of the disparate elements above constitute what people think of as a digital camera, since, as we know from the relatively limited qualitative research on practices, digital camera users routinely cite these technological features as integral to processes of image capture, selection, storage and display (Lee 2009; Van House et al. 2004; Van House 2011). In line with the above, during the mid-2000s many consumers had both analogue and digital cameras and often differentiated between them in terms of how specific material features of each shaped the subjects and situations for which they were used. For example, Van House and her colleagues (2004) showed how shutter speed was considered 'too slow' on the digital for 'candid' shots, the interchangeable lenses for film cameras were beneficial for serious shots, and the lightweight nature of digital point and shoots made them a permanent accessory, with film being reserved for special occasions. These trends have shifted in line with further developments in camera technology, with digital SLR cameras now effectively mimicking their earlier film counterparts. As such, people now often have multiple *digital* cameras, reproducing this previous film/digital distinction between the serious and the everyday.

Of course, one unequivocal material shift is that film cameras are for the most part no longer manufactured or available to buy. Some people still use both, although it is increasingly difficult to purchase rolls of film, to locate a darkroom, or to update old equipment. Where film cameras are no longer used they have sometimes become memory objects in their own right, valued for their signification of another time:

> I have never picked it up; it still has film in it, which wouldn't be good any more. It had a roll of film in it, a brand new roll of film in it, because I always made sure it had a roll of film in it ready to go. Yeah, I haven't picked it up since I got that. But I do wish I had the camera that my grandmother gave me in grade 6 – the 110, cause I'm a pack rat, and normally I keep everything, and I remember I threw out that 110 . . . remember the 110? I threw it out because I finally said to myself, 'Okay you're not gonna use this', because I would know that photography is such a big part of me I would make my woodworking husband make me a display, and I would display the cameras that I've had through the years. (A, legal secretary)

> And one day, I was getting some film . . . I can't remember what happened – either they were out, or, as I bought it, the man said 'We're having trouble getting this stuff now', he said, 'cause so few people are using it.' And that got me scared. I said, you know what's going to happen. I'm gonna end up with these cameras and there's not going to be any film for them. (X, retired)

In such cases it is the combination of the apparent benefits of digital cameras – particularly portability, immediacy and lack of production cost – alongside the disappearance of the materials required to do film photography that have solidified the presence of digital in popular practice.

There is nothing about the materiality of the digital camera that makes it more mobile than a point and shoot film camera. Nonetheless, research has shown that vast numbers of people take their digital cameras (not just cellphones with imaging capabilities) with them at all times (see Van House 2011 for an overview). The ubiquity of the digital camera seems to be tied to a *sense* of its immediacy. In turn, the broader notion of immediacy – of capturing and communicating moments as they occur – relies to some extent on the ability to have the camera with you at all times, which has itself become a completely ordinary aspect of 'mobile lives' (Elliott and Urry 2010). The difference between film and digital has been, for some, a transition from 'heavy' to 'light', as they have adopted what they see as the point and shoot *nature* of digital photography, which has reconfigured the kind of photography in which they engage:

> I don't think there's a difference in how you frame the shot – you know, in how you focus it, what you're choosing to take the picture of. To me they're apples and apples. I don't see any difference with that. The cameras are, in terms of technology now, they are very comparable, I think. The digital cameras are very sophisticated now. So, and in fact I think you can even do more in terms of taking a picture. You can do more with a digital point and shoot than you can do with a film. I got away from taking pictures because my camera's very heavy and I didn't enjoy . . . because my 35 mm film, my original one was completely manual, so it was making me nuts! Every time I got it set the victim was long gone. Now, so then I decided that a digital point and shoot is what I wanted because it was light and quick, and I could just do what I want to do, always on auto, see you later. (S, physician)

The difference here is that film-based point and shoot cameras were considered relatively basic in their capabilities. Digital cameras in the 2000s have combined the immediacy and ease of the point and shoot while at the same time translating previously manual processes into the camera and the various levels of immediate operation alluded to earlier. In other words, immediacy has come to describe almost every aspect of the technology and the practice. For many people, it is the immediacy of the image-making process that has led to their adoption of the digital rather than the film SLR:

You don't have to wait. I don't like waiting. So the idea of taking my 35 mm, and again now wanting to get into different lenses, and wanting to get into what I would perceive as, like, real photography kind of stuff, I needed to get away. I wanted to add lenses, so that's why I went to the Canon, and again the Rebel came out before Nikon came out with their digital SLR. So I just went with what was current, what was there that I could afford. So the digital . . . so I did, once I jumped I traded my film one in on the digital. I traded in my 35 mm film; I don't have any film anywhere now. (F, museum curator)

These material aspects of the digital camera have enabled it to become a *routine* accessory within an exponentially increasing range of social situations. This is highly significant, as it almost necessarily implies a shift in the parameters of what images actually get made. We know – both anecdotally and in terms of research – there are vastly more digital images made than there were with film. There are several sociotechnically driven reasons for this. Many more people have digital cameras than had film cameras (for example, where there may have been one film camera per household, it is now more common for each member of the family to have a digital camera of some sort, and, crucially, this includes children), they are present more often than film cameras ever were, and they allow for more images to be taken. Further to this, research has shown that the range of images made has shifted as a result. While the same kinds of images are taken (special events, and so on) as with film, this has expanded to include the mundane on a scale hitherto not realized (Murray 2008). In chapter 3, I showed how there is a difference between considering digital photos such as these as ephemeral or mundane and yet highly *valued*. I also showed how novel problems of originality arise when there are just so many images being produced. In terms of technology, there are several ways in which digital cameras in their own right have altered the very idea of what counts as a photo. Most obviously, the ease with which high-quality images can be produced, reframed, cropped, adjusted and deleted within the camera creates a casual sensibility about making vast numbers of images, regardless of what people intend to do with them:

> But I just find the film . . . see, my older sister wanted a camera, but she had no desire – 'I don't want digital, I don't want digital, I don't want digital' – so we got her the film thing, and now that's going to sit because somebody else gave her a little point and shoot and now she's . . . it's again that satisfaction of seeing it right away and if you don't like it take it again. She's very particular about . . . as opposed to I get very, very, very nonchalant about how I take, because I know I can crop and pick out, you know, (E, student)

> I've got stuff in my camera right now. I probably have thirty pictures in a row, none of which I want to keep, but I haven't bothered deleting them. Sometimes, when I take pictures of birds out here, I'll just shoot several as the bird moves. I'll shoot several, knowing that only one will be worth keeping. But I haven't deleted them yet, until I need the card cleared and need more space. (X, administrator)

For those who are using their digital cameras to reproduce aspects of film photography, in the sense intimated above with nature-orientated photography, the camera's ability to store, view or delete hundreds of images alters the temporality of photographic practice but not necessarily the subject matter of the images. For people using point and shoot digital cameras (or cameraphones) the subject matter has unquestionably altered as a result. As Van House argues, the carrying of a digital image-capture device most of the time has encouraged many people to 'see the world as a field of potential images' (2011: 131). The huge production of digital photos as a result of the ubiquitous presence of the camera (and vice versa, of course) creates a range of subsequent issues about meaning and classification that will be explored in chapter 5.

In discussing the historical developments, narrative positioning and uses of digital cameras above it should be observed that these are not isolated aspects of technology and culture but are mutually constitutive. In what follows I want to examine in more detail how these processes, from the point of view of science and technology studies, are reconfiguring the relations between non-human camera and human photographer in terms of how agency is redistributed. This is having consequences for current understandings of how consumers stand in relation to photographic practice and digital cultural practices more widely.

The redistribution of photographic agency

As discussed above, cultural expectations about digital photography have been generated and shaped by changes in camera technology, the advertising strategies of manufacturers, popular discourses of promise and threat, and the ways in which people engage and enact all of this through patterns of use. Manufacturers (e.g., Kodak) have often claimed that digital cameras will 'make you a better photographer', with this notion eventually being promoted within publications such as *Popular Photography* from the 2000s. But, as observed so far, one of the most important aspects of the digital camera is how it makes an array of complex processes associated with analogue photography invisible to the user. It would seem that the skills associated with film photography, from framing shots to processing photographs, have been incorporated *into* the digital camera. Have these skills simply been lost? Have they been replaced with 'digital skills'? Is ubiquitous photography a more democratic set of practices but devoid of *craft*?

Quickening and experimentation
The digital camera's incorporation of previously external processes rearranges the relationships between camera and photographer, closing down some opportunities for human intervention while opening up others. A typical range of digital SLR cameras currently on the market are likely to have

technical features that used to be thought of as *skills*. The Nikon D90, for example, has a 'scene recognition system' that evaluates the images you make in comparison to an in-built database of 30,000 photographic scenes, enabling the camera to calculate the 'accurate exposure' required. The in-built lighting system analyses shadows and highlights in specific images, 'taming high-contrast situations in real time'. The three alternative focus modes provide the photographer with pre-established ways of focusing a shot; for example, one of these is a 'face priority' mode. These now commonplace processes are occurring in the camera rather than being calculated by the photographer in conjunction with the camera, and in this way represent a realignment of human and non-human agency.

There are two key ways in which the demonstrable skills of the photographer are altered by this process: firstly, through quickening the accumulation of tacit knowledge (which may previously have taken years) and, secondly, in enabling new forms of experimentation to become ordinary aspects of the practice:

> I get more practice. You just keep clicking and practising without it costing a huge amount of money. And the costing is a huge thing for me . . . cause it was expensive . . . I would definitely experiment more if I had more time. Basically, I think it's that I'm taking more pictures and of more things. And probably taking some that I just sort of more freely without thinking twice, because it doesn't really matter. (C, nurse)

People usually make reference to the 'lack of waste' in digital photography, articulating a sense of how disposability and deletion allow them rapidly to accumulate creative skills. In this sense, the digital camera acts as a *technology of skill redistribution* rather than de-skilling. The specificities of framing, lighting, and so on, are developed over a different temporal period enabled by the camera, rather than having to be embodied in the photographer prior to the act of image-making.

> I think what's happened is I still take a phenomenal amount of pictures, but it doesn't cost us so much, which was a factor. So I still have 800 pictures of pelicans from Mexico but, you know, I don't have a hard copy of them. It has . . . and enables me to experiment a bit more that I can take ten pictures of the pelican doing this, and if I don't like a couple of them I can get rid of them, and it's not going to be such an outlay and such a waste. So it's enabled me to be a bit more creative, I think. (S, stage manager)

The most common immediate justification for this among photographers is economics. As we have seen, this has the potential to change what counts as a 'good image' and also the subject matter of ordinary photography, both of which subsequently have their own cultural trajectories as reproducible conventions. Similar shifts occurred with the rise of the snapshot outlined earlier, but these have been intensified through the digital camera's potentially endless sequential use:

> I think the only subjects that are slightly altered are the fact that we can now get close-ups better with this camera than the other one. It's clearer I can take more pictures of nature and bugs. So I maybe take more of those, but I think it has increased my . . . my sort of ability to take risk. I can take . . . I can try a few different things and it doesn't matter. (S, stage manager)

This difference in this specific sense between the film and digital camera is directly comparable to the shift from wet- to dry-plate photography, and has similar implications for the established boundaries between the abstract categories of amateur and professional, which are themselves initially the product of manufacturing and advertising but, more importantly, become part of the *doing* of photographic practice on the ground (Bourdieu 1990b). The ability to accumulate the skill previously associated with professional photography is a common theme among amateur enthusiasts, but is not always positioned positively among those who see themselves as *serious* amateurs. For example, there is often an ambivalence or uneasiness about how the digital camera has levels of automation that appeared previously to be a matter of human agency or choice, and that this is changing the subjectivity of the photographer and their ability to demonstrate skill across the fuller range of photographic practice:

> With film, well you've gotta be mindful of cost. Not so much just with cost but the fact that I've got . . . you've say I've got three rolls of films, that means I have 108 pictures, 108 frames. I can't afford to just go click, click, click. You've got to be more selective. Now I think it makes you a better photographer, a more thoughtful photographer, and makes you plan ahead. I think one thing about digital – I think digital, for me at least, is making me sloppy. I don't have to think. I just shoot, shoot, shoot, and I'll select later. I don't think that's a good way . . . and also the automatic features of the cameras. You see my cameras have never been automatic. (X, administrator)

> I used to use a hand-held [light] meter. I still have my hand-held meter and um . . . and you get to know on any given day, given your film speed, the kind of light you got, you get to know what a good exposure is. Like, I can tell you right now, if I was shooting ah . . . they call it ISO now – it used to be called ASA film speed. But if I was shooting a film with a speed of, say, 200, which is a very popular speed for colour film, if I was shooting a speed of 200 today I would shoot, let's say, 1/50th and between F8 and F11. You see, the way you do it is you take the reciprocal of your film speed as your shutter speed, and on a bright sunny day, totally unclouded sunny day, bright sunshine, you take the reciprocal of your film speed and F16. But then, of course, you know how film speed works with the shutter speed. (X, administrator)

A central dimension of this redistribution of skills between camera (and related technologies) and photographer is that it is gendered and follows social and cultural (class) distinctions. The boundaries between amateur and professional have been explicitly gendered historically, with (at the simplest level) 'complex' cameras being aimed at male (professional) photographers and 'snapshot' cameras aimed at female (amateur) photographers. More specifically, within amateur photography itself, the production of photographs has been associated with men and the business of narrative construction (albums and display) associated with women. In this latter regard, female engagement with amateur or personal photography has been associated largely with constructing narratives of family history and daily life, particularly the capture of key moments in the life course of a family unit (birthdays, weddings, holidays, graduation), representing notions of unity, happiness and successful forms of family life (Spence and Holland 1991; Slater 1995). In this sense, *competent* amateur practice has often been defined in these technical and cultural terms: the ability to represent ideals of family, self and the past, which can also be displayed and viewed as permanent or autonomous representations of reality. The notion that this is a skill with demonstrable cultural capital attached to it was reinforced during the twentieth century in popular photography publications but also, and perhaps more significantly, in key representations of competent domestic practice, such as *Good Housekeeping*. The simplistic theme of democratization within popular discourses of digital photography disguises how current practices are gendered and classed in ways that both reproduce and break with analogue photographic practice. The simple story is one of an association between computerization and photography and the subsequent 'de-feminization' of album-making. The more complex story is one of multiply anchored gendered practices, related to the individualization of the production and consumption of images, the rise of 'prosumptive' image management practices, and the underlying redefinition of consumer markets by manufacturers and marketers.

Individualization and privatization
One of the most significant changes in the ways in which popular or personal photography is conducted is the

individualization or privatization of the production process. In a sense, the film camera was an isolated device but, for most amateur photographers, once the film was complete, the process of producing prints was handed over to developers, often available in the high street or mall. This differentiation of the image-making and developing processes has now been reversed, with personal digital photographers now responsible for the entire production process. The process is individualized via the camera and its connection to advanced editing and organizational software, such as Photoshop or Photoshop Elements, or the standard iPhoto, in what has become known as the 'digital darkroom'. Presented 'empowering' the user, the perceived ease of the process is important for the notion that categories of amateur and professional have again become significantly blurred. The separation of production and consumption of the image for most amateurs structured the development of visual literacy in ways that the digital camera negates (Cobley and Haeffner 2009):

> That's what was really annoying, because you'd take the one and then you'd wait for the film to come back and be totally ticked because you've lost the opportunity, you've lost the picture, and it's crap and . . . or it doesn't even get developed. Right, it's so bad that they can't even . . . you can't tell anything with the film until it comes back to you. Your digital camera's basically free once you get . . . you know, it doesn't cost me 1 cent to take 800 pictures tomorrow. (H, student)

This might be conceptualized in a number of ways. Firstly, it can be considered a democratization of image-making, in that the conventions governing the production of images (which may or may not end up in printed form) are apparently arbitrary and subject to individual taste rather than the criteria of professional developers. Secondly, this might be taken further and seen as an example of so-called digital creativity – the idea that digital content is increasingly produced by greater numbers of consumers without the intervention of gatekeepers, such as developers, or other producers, such as film development companies. Thirdly, we might think about the invention of a whole new set of skills and forms of expertise, related to Photoshop and associated software for performing this kind of production. Making, storing, manipulating and distributing are at the very least overlapping processes which can be performed with levels of immediacy unimaginable to photographers of the nineteenth and twentieth centuries. For many within the semi-professional and serious amateur communities, such a development has been a matter of the final triumph of automation in photographic practice. But it is worth considering what new skills are generated and how the skills of the photographer have been redistributed through the changing configurations of technologies that make up digital photographic practice. The initial consumer-level forms of digital photography involved the printing of digital images from the camera, usually via a PC and printer. It is often assumed or stated that, with the increasing use of online forums for storing, viewing and distributing digital photos, most images are not printed. This is probably true, but such a fact disguises some important recent shifts that relate both to producer-led efforts to reposition printing via dramatically improved technologies and to the interrelation between digital cameras, other technical systems and emerging forms of consumer-orientated cultural production.

Convergent systems and devices

The changing role of the camera in the redistribution of skill and agency outlined above also stems from the connection of cameras in one way or another to information systems. The camera, whatever its apparently specific characteristics, has always been a relational device – a relay within broader networks or sociotechnical systems which mutually constitute its attributes, its meaning and the relative agency of the constituent elements of photographic practice (Shove et al. 2007). The range of possible elements with which the camera can now be connected is vast, dynamic and diverse. The camera can be connected to memory sticks, printers, laptops, PCs, Wi-Fi networks, other cameras, websites, and so on, in any number of combinations, each of which enables different processes and practices to be constituted *through* them. In this sense, the potential trajectories of photographic practice are immensely variable and context-dependent.

Even if we consider just the relations between the camera and the internet, the convergence of visual, computing and telecommunications technologies has produced a vast architecture for practices of digital photography and at the same time repositions the camera as a node in a qualitatively different kind of network than that of the late nineteenth or the twentieth century. As Victor Keegan observes:

> It is difficult to know these days whether the internet is reinventing photography or vice versa. The convergence of cheap digital cameras, affordable computers and low-cost access to the internet has made photography vastly more popular than it has ever been and transformed it from a personal to a community experience. (Keegan 2006)

There is nothing new about convergence in photographic culture. Photography has always been intertwined with other media technologies, most obviously if we consider where most photographs are actually viewed – in magazines, newspapers, and so on. The convergence of photographic images with print technologies radically altered both (Tagg 1988), and, as observed at the beginning of this chapter, it was the convergence of photography within new communications networks in the late nineteenth century that enabled its transformation into the dominant visual technology of modernity. The observation that photographic practice requires technologies to be configured in relation to each other suggests that attention is paid to the specificity of those configurations. It is especially important to note that conventional and novel arrangements are equally possible when technologies are reconfigured. For example, many people use just a camera and a printer, where others never use printers and use only web-based storage platforms or look at images on hand-held devices, and so on.

With this in mind, there are two key forms of technological convergence to be discussed here: firstly, how the location of the digital camera within increasingly complex ecosystems or suites of technologies has enabled some extensions of photographic practice to emerge in the context of prosumer capitalism and, secondly, how the disappearance of the camera inside other technologies such as cameraphones has refigured the camera as the key technology of citizen journalism.

Evolving systems

In the summer of 2011, Apple announced the imminent arrival of the iCloud:

> the effortless way to access just about everything on all your devices. iCloud stores your content so it's always accessible from your iPad, iPhone, iPod touch, Mac, or PC. It gives you instant access to your music, apps, latest photos, and more. And it keeps your email, contacts, and calendars up to date across all your devices. (www.apple.com/icloud/what-is. html)

There are a number of significant issues raised by this description. Firstly, it is a further indication that software systems – particularly those that automatically organize content in the name of ease – are becoming important agents in framing the possibilities of practice. Secondly, it demonstrates how normal it has become in affluent regions of the world to acquire a suite of devices through which it is *expected* that cultural content (photos, conversation, music, etc.) will seamlessly move. This is an example of the *explicitation* of what were previously implied relationships between technologies and practices, or of how 'technology is society made durable' (Latour 1991). As argued in chapter 2, devices are always constituted through broader suites of technologies (Shove et al.

2007) of which they are part, but often this is not immediately visible, and it certainly requires more 'work' to produce interoperability than in the case of the Apple ecosystem in which such reciprocity is designed.

In this way the properties and agency of the digital camera should be understood as the outcome of a shifting network of 'allies', the normalization of which would enable and constrain practices significantly. For example, during the 1990s it was thought that PCs, television and DVDs would be the key allies of the digital camera for *displaying* photos in new ways. Since then there have been evolving relationships between such suites of technologies – cameras and computers, memory cards, laptops, web-based platforms, Wi-Fi networks, and so on – which have enabled digital photography to become as much about image distribution, manipulation and management in their own right as about modes of display (van Dijck 2011).

This has enabled the stabilization of several trajectories that position digital photography in terms of 'prosumption' – the idea that consumers have either become more professional in their consumption, perhaps creating content and taking control over parts of the production process, or increasingly engaged in the labouring of cultural production through consumption practices. For example, Lister and his colleagues (2009: 33) suggest that many of the specialist skills involved in media production during the twentieth century have 'become more generally dispersed throughout the population as a whole, in the form of a widening baseline of "computer literacy", information technology skills, and especially the availability of software that increasingly affords the production of "user-generated content"'. They go on to suggest, following Rubenstein and Sluis (2008), that domestic photography has 'been transformed' through the configuration of cameras, post-production processes, and distribution networks. An example of how this contributes to the blurring of the boundaries between professionals and amateurs is that snapshot hobbyists, serious amateurs and professionals all post photos on Flickr, and it can often be difficult to tell the difference between the latter two groups, since most people do not self-identify (Murray 2008: 155). Further to this, there are other ways in which evolving systems of technologies are enabling novel forms of individual and collective practice to emerge.

The current prominence of geolocational technologies, discussed earlier, has been promoted as prosumptive through, to take one example, Microsoft's Photosynth, developed in partnership with NASA, which invites consumers to 'use your camera to stitch the world'. People can use this software to conjoin multiple images of specific objects or places in order to create 'synths' – 3D visual representations through which an object or place can be seen from any angle. This involves the software sifting images for similarities and calculating the position from which each one was taken in relation to the subject and then forming a composite and 'interactive panorama' on screen. The result can be distributed on the Web by individual users and uploaded to mapping sites that allow others to look at 3D representations of specific spaces and places that are geotagged. That the consumer production of panoramic environments has become a standard aspect of commercial mapping technologies positions digital cameras as important relays in the production and consumption of the geotagged visual landscape. In this way, the historical intertextuality of photography is taking novel forms, appropriating and then requiring new skills previously associated with professional computing.

A second, rather different example is the intersection of cameras and craft-orientated websites that invite consumers to make things from their photos. Indeed, digital photos have become key resources of 'craft consumption' (Campbell 2005), in which consumers produce new commodities from combinations of existing ones. For example, www.shutterfly. com enables consumers to upload digital photos and then materialize them in photo books, cards and other stationery, and web pages, by providing both an image storage service and the ability to purchase commodities that use these images, while www.snapfish.com offers a similar service and a huge range of 'personalized objects' that use individual images uploaded by the consumer. Other sites offer massive repositories of professional and amateur images, which can generate royalties for the producer if their photos are used by others. The largest of these – www.webshots.com – is indicative of the ways in which amateur and professional categories have been blurred through the commodification of both as digital stock. In each case, these companies bring together the results of personal photographic practice and the commercial production of visually orientated commodities. On the one hand, there is not necessarily anything new about using personal photos for decorating existing objects, producing new ones or commodifying specific images. On the other hand, the transformation of traditional craft practices or modes of exchange into large networked commercial enterprises has established digital photography as a significant prosumer technology, contributing to its very ubiquity.

A similar trajectory is promoted within mainstream journalism, where consumer-citizens are asked to provide their 'voice' through the uploading of personal photos. For example, the BBC has a service called 'Your news, your pictures', which asks people to upload personal photos of significant events, as 'News can happen anywhere at any time, and we want you to be our eyes'. Similarly, CBC News has a Flickr photo stream – CBC Community pictures – that again promotes the notion of (adding) 'your voice' through the uploading of digital photos.

These developments illustrate how the technical systems within which the digital camera is situated have evolved in the cultural context of consumer capitalism. These are all significant examples of how personal photography appears to have far greater cultural capital than it once did in the redrawing of the boundary between amateur and professional in favour of the prosumer or consumer-citizen. Subsequently, we can also see how this involves the unpaid use of consumer labour to produce the cultural content of contemporary craft and news industries. This ambivalence exemplifies the contradictions of the notion of prosumption that, rather than its dissolution, involve a reassembling of the relation between production and consumption through sociotechnical systems, which may or may not be democratic. They also highlight the ways in which digital cameras have been repositioned in relation to other media, enabling novel configurations of camera, photographer and image and intensifying the movement of photos through related sociotechnical systems.

The convergence of sociotechnical forms has arguably become more complex and faster over the last ten years or so, especially when we consider the rise of the hand-held computing device. The convergences of image-capture devices with cellphones has enabled a very different kind of photography to emerge – a form inextricably tied to the web and a host of other processes and devices.

Disappearing cameras

It has been argued that the most important development in camera technology over the last ten years has been the cameraphone (see Goggin 2006), which in a sense entails the *disappearance* of the camera as conventionally understood. The rate of adoption of cameraphones is significant in its own right:

> This is a seminal time for cameraphones. Within the next few months, according to industry calculations, the number of cameraphones is expected to exceed the total number of conventional cameras ever sold. Not bad for a device less than 10 years old, as cameras have been around for a century. (Keegan 2008)

It is estimated that nearly 1 billion cameraphones had been sold by the end of 2011, illustrating the increasing prominence of telecommunications industries in digital photography and certainly altering the possibilities and parameters of image-making in everyday life. Cameras now appear in phones and smartphones, phones merge with iPods to make iPhones, Wi-Fi appears in cameras, projectors appear in cameraphones, every device is web-enabled, and so on. This movement of the camera *into* other technologies – most notably the cell or mobile phone, but also the laptop and tablet – has involved the convergence of photography and communication in a technically descriptive sense, with camera technology becoming an industry standard:

> These days, the very idea of a mobile without camera or video facility seems absurd. They're more portable than most digital cameras and, more importantly, offer faster connection with the Internet, which is a key consideration in this age of virtual presenteeism. (Jeffries 2010)

The prevalence of digital devices such as these in everyday life is shaping the ways in which digital photography can be practised. For example, Elliott and Urry (2010: 28) developed the concept of 'miniaturized mobilities' to explain the dynamics of 'life on the move', shaped and made possible through myriad mobile devices and software systems. A number of novel social patterns are generated – mobile connectivity, continuous coordination, strategic scheduling, and the negotiation of sociabilities through patterns of presence and absence. In terms of the cameraphone or smartphone, the ability to make, store, send and receive photos regardless of where and when people are allows for the integration of photography with these other patterns of mobile communication (see also Castells 2010; Ling and Donner 2009).

What happens when digital cameras become *unavoidable* in this way? Digital photos are clearly implicated in the practice of 'retrieving affect' that Elliot and Urry (2010: 33) describe, whereby affective feelings can be produced through mobile devices when other modes of connection are absent (looking at digital photos when away from home, for example). In more detail, in several studies of how cameraphones are being used, Van House and her colleagues (2005) have observed both enduring and novel practices of image-making and distribution emerging. Cameraphone images are used for sharing, memory and self-expressive purposes in similar ways to other photos, but each of these is extended in novel ways, partly in relation to the dynamics of mobile digital devices but also due to the more specific image capacity of the cellphone. For example, given the ubiquity and mobility of the cameraphone and its reduced picture quality, it is perhaps not surprisingly used for mundane images of daily life and 'functional' images in the form of capturing text (Van House 2007). Similarly, while photos have often been shared, the sharing of cameraphone images is implied by the device (as a communications technology) and its use as an 'affective' technology, with 'playful self-expression' also being extended, as it is considered a less serious technology than a camera (it can be speculated that this dominates the use of the laptop camera). The frequency of image-taking is significantly enhanced by the embedding of the camera in the cellphone, and now the smartphone, while at the same time many users do not consider this to 'photography' (ibid.). In line with this, in terms of the images made, others have argued that the cameraphone makes photography more thoroughly ordinary in that, because of the cellphone's constant presence, the everyday is necessarily *privileged* over the iconic:

> In comparison to the traditional camera, which gets trotted out for special excursions and events – noteworthy moments bracketed off from the mundane – camera phones capture the more fleeting and unexpected moments of surprise, beauty and adoration in the everyday. (Daisuke and Ito 2003)

The novelty of the cameraphone exists in tandem with more traditional uses of the camera. One way in which this occurs is in the production of the most ordinary images but their immediate potential mobility through global telecommunications networks. The London Tube bombings (2005), alluded to in chapter 1, remain the quintessential case of the efficacy of the cellphone image. In contrast to the idea that cellphone photography isn't really photographic, it is the poor quality, grainy images that have exemplified the continued salience of the photographic in contemporary news reporting and citizen-journalism. This observation simply reminds us that, in terms of the abstracted image, there is nothing new per se in its aesthetic dimensions or the fact that it can become iconic. Indeed, although involving moving images, the familiar 8 mm colour home movie that Abraham Zapruder took in Dallas on 22 November 1963, capturing the assassination of President Kennedy, is similar in aesthetics to the camera-phone footage taken of Saddam Hussein's execution. Both these have become iconic in their grainy authenticity. But the second example exemplifies the key differences here, which are not about digital images as such, but about the technical systems within which they are made and between which they are able to migrate.

Firstly, it is not only the small size of the cellphone but also the fact that *it is not a camera* that makes it a potentially ubiquitous imaging device even within the most 'secured' of situations. In this sense, its physical aspects and the apparent practical necessity of having a cellphone position it as the key technology of citizen journalism, capable of slipping into unlikely situations and capturing the serendipitous, the accidental or the unexpected. Secondly, the aforementioned possibilities of networking are *stabilized* with the cellphone in its dominant capacity as necessarily configured with communication networks, allowing for the rapid, 'viral' and sometimes uncontrollable migration of images across the globe in seconds. As suggested earlier, the rise of digital photography is inseparable from the practices and expectations of contemporary photojournalism, in terms of the ethics of malleability and the material dimensions of the camera. Accordingly, the most significant effect of the cameraphone has arguably been seen within this profession, where the categories of 'journalist' and 'citizen' have been deeply problematized:

> The digital camera is an egalitarian piece of technology – cheap (most mobile phones have them), easy to use, convenient to carry and quick to produce images that can be spread throughout cyberspace in seconds. What we are witnessing, as any professional photojournalist will tell you, is the unstoppable rise of the citizen-photographer. (Jack 2009)

It is likely to be the case that greater capacity for moving images on the cellphone and other mobile digital devices will shape the future of visual citizen journalism, alongside the increased use of Twitter and other textual social media. Nonetheless, the dual processes of reconfiguration examined above – the evolving sociotechnical systems within which the camera is situated, and the insertion of camera technology inside mobile digital devices – have been and remain central in redefining both camera, photographer and image in relation to one another and central aspects of photographic, journalistic and consumer practice.

Concluding remarks

This chapter has sought heuristically to downplay the image in digital photography in favour of technologies and systems and their relationship to changing conventions of skill and practice. This may seem counter-intuitive, especially to students of photography perhaps, but it has hopefully made it clear that changes in the way images are produced, consumed and distributed are made possible by the dynamics of technologies and how they frame (but not determine) the possibilities of photographic practice. I have continued to draw upon ideas in science and technology studies in order to examine three kinds of related *reconfiguration* – of the camera, of the photographer and of the image.

The stand-alone digital camera retains many features of earlier cameras, perhaps most importantly the lens, but has 'condensed' (Hand and Shove 2007) many aspects of previous practices by incorporating several novel features which generate the quickening of conventional photographic skills, the development of digital visual literacy, and novel cultural expectations about immediacy, portability and convenience. Aside from the hyped promises of advertising, all of these things have enabled the camera to be used by far more people than ever before – in effect producing new kinds of photographers and destabilizing the boundaries of serious and amateur that were historically shaped by class, gender and convention. The convergence of the camera with other technical devices and systems, in tandem with the transformation of cameras within communications devices, has allowed exponentially more and increasingly varied kinds of images to be generated in an increasing number of situations, the trajectories of which have become radically ambivalent.

The discussions above have been underpinned by the notion that relationships between technology and practice can be seen as 'co-evolutionary', where changes in technology produce new expectations and vice versa. As a corrective to causally determinist accounts, I have illustrated how some of the cultural conventions of photography often remain intact and have been important in shaping the reception and uses of these new technologies. During the 1990s and early 2000s there was a *duality* of analogue and digital within industry and advertising, and often among individual practitioners. Digital cameras of one kind or another have now almost completely supplanted their analogue counterparts, reproducing many aspects of earlier practice, but have also become very different sociotechnical entities, enabling novel trajectories to emerge. The impact of this transition upon those most significant of practices – memory practices – will be explored in the next chapter.

CHAPTER FIVE

Memory and Classification: Between the Album and the Tag Cloud

Introduction

This chapter focuses upon practices of personal digital photography in relation to the themes of memory and classification. In the previous chapter I showed how changes in the technological architecture of digital photography within which the camera is situated enables a diversification of what counts as photography, who gets to practise it and how. I drew particular attention to the redistribution of agency and photographic skill through new configurations of photographer, camera, and associated hardware and software of image production and consumption. I emphasized the significance of the digital camera in its many variants here: cameras can now recognize smiles, make aesthetic judgements, and know the spatiotemporal location of image capture. When coupled with organizational software or web-based distribution systems, the ways in which digital images can migrate from one material context to another appear boundless. These attributes can be usefully considered in relation to memory and the ways in which images are framed, classified, stored and retrieved by combinations of humans, cameras and the many technical systems within which they are configured. The materials and social practices of photography have always been associated with making and sharing memories, or at least with remembrance in a general sense (Barthes 1982; Sontag 1977). This chapter explores the ways in which established practices of photographic memory-making, classification, storage and retrieval are altering through digitization.

Pulling together several themes explored so far, I will show how digital photography both reproduces and transforms some of the relationships between photography and individual and collective memory-making. The mundanity of ubiquitous photography that has been examined in terms of the digital image and the technologies that enable it raises the most obvious question about what will be remembered, how and why. The potential relationships between ordinary photographic practice and the collective memory of the archive have arguably become more visible and explicit in contemporary theories of memory, in conjunction with the emergence of 'archives of everyday life' (Featherstone 2000) such as Flickr, Photobucket, Facebook, YouTube, and so on. The ways in which the technical architecture of digital photography often promotes the *distribution* rather than the fixing of images above all else is an especially important component of new modes of classification and potential memory. The often underestimated yet crucial point is that forms of distribution made available through cameras, cellphones, smartphones and web-based photo-sharing sites are at the same time modes of storage and classification. Some have argued that these are radically different from previous album-based collections, which remained fixed and linear in their relations. For example, Murray (2008) shows how the architecture of Flickr promotes a form of photography 'in motion', arguing that photo streams *promote* the temporariness of photos, always replaceable by others. Moreover, the issue of malleability, at the level of both individual images and the cultural acceptability of transformation, takes on a rather different role here, where, according to Bowker, 'Our past has always been malleable, but now it is malleable with a new viscosity' (2005: 5). In line with these initial observations, this chapter explores aspects of these emerging systems and practices at the level of personal photography in the following ways.

Firstly, I will explain how photography is central to social and cultural theories and practices of memory. There is a broad consensus among scholars that the shift from ana-logue to digital technologies in the sphere of photography has potentially profound implications for memory-making at the present time and in the future, especially if communicative practices are indeed being prioritized over practices of pres-ervation in the ways that recent research suggests (Murray 2008; Rubenstein and Sluis 2008; van Dijck 2011).

Secondly, in order to provide a grounded context, I will revisit studies of album-making in the domestic sphere in order to ask what is continuous and discontinuous after digi-tization, with particular attention paid to the ways in which photos are organized, stored, viewed and shared in domestic environments. The key question here is whether the imme-diacy and disposability of the digital image discussed in previous chapters changes how it is positioned in relation to personal strategies of classification, meaning organization and memory-making. I will show how the sheer volume of digital images being made in or anchored to the domestic sphere is producing novel problems of organization, includ-ing the emergence of parallel personal archives, changing relationships between different storage media, and anxieties about digital loss. The photo album, which defined photo-graphic order and memory during the twentieth century, is not only a domestic 'family' technology but has been central to professional and amateur collections in general and, as such, links individual to collective memory-making. I will show how the album, as a mode of classification, is not in fact disappear-ing but is being reconfigured in several ways.

Thirdly, building upon the previous chapter, I will discuss how the exponential growth of photo-sharing platforms and social networking environments is enabling new conjunctions of photography and classification to emerge that potentially radically reposition personal memory in relation to collec-tive memory. The intended and unintended distribution of photos through social media will be explored, focusing specifi-cally upon tagging and classification processes in Facebook.

I will show that the relative significance of social practices and algorithmic processes enabled by software in ordering and distributing digital photos is shaping the ways in which people take, upload, classify and 'manage' images, and in addition raises more profound questions for ethical conduct in contemporary visual culture.

Photography, memory and classification

> The traditional idea of collective memory is generally grounded in the presumption that the individual and the collective are separate entities that are associated *through* technological mechanisms, such as media, and *through* social institutions, such as archives. However, the formation of memory is increasingly structured *by* digital networks, and memory's constituting agency is both technological and human. (van Dijck 2011: 2)

Memory practices are embedded within historically specific cultural frameworks which are themselves made possible by objects, technologies and other devices (Brockmeier 2010). Acts or practices of remembering involve delegating work to technological devices and systems, whether the diary, the printed word, the taxonomical classification, the library catalogue, the post-it note or the photograph. The photographic image is an important component of memory-making regardless of whether it is intended as such when made. This has been true at a variety of scales, each of which necessarily involves the sociotechnical construction of memory. For example, the memories of nation-states are collated and produced in national archives, many of which contain vast photographic representations of what are deemed to be significant and relevant events. These are collated, preserved, ordered and made retrievable according to specific regimes of classification that shape the possibilities of memory (Bowker 2005; Hand 2008). The memories of specific families are often documented photographically in the family album, retrospectively collating or indeed constructing family histories for future and perhaps as yet unknown relatives and friends. The conventions of domestic album-making are similarly anchored in specific modes of classification, most commonly organized chronologically around events. One of the key questions in contemporary memory studies is whether the modern relationship between photography and memory, typified perhaps by the apparent fixity and durability of the archive and the album, is deeply and fundamentally challenged by the *mobilities* of information culture.

The proliferation of visual traces stemming from ubiquitous photography would seem to exemplify the notion that contemporary societies seek to remember as never before. In relation to this, there is a growing academic interest and literature on the social, historical and political aspects of memory, particularly at the level of the nation-state or society. Much of this concerns broad issues of commemoration, monuments, reparations, tourism, and so on, especially in light of postmodernization after the Second World War (Urry 2002). The sociological study of memory has encompassed the selective nature of collective memory (Halbwachs 1992), the gendered nature of memory and identity (Spence and Holland 1991), relationships between social memory and temporality (Jedlowski 2001) and the dialogic re-evaluation of established cultural memories (Olick 2007), among other orientations. At the level of everyday life, it has been argued that 'Every attic is an archive, every living room a museum. Never before has so much been recorded, collected; and never before has remembering been so compulsive' (Gillis 1994: 14). While yielding important insights about the contested and *negotiated* nature of memory practices, this work has largely underplayed the constitutive or performative roles of technologies and conventions of classification regimes in *actively* shaping remembrance (Bowker 2005).

By contrast, scholars in the information sciences, science and technology studies, and media and communications have emphasized several important trajectories in the relationships between technology and memory which are relevant for thinking about the ubiquity of photography. Firstly, the digitization of visual and textual objects and interaction in daily life (photography, email, instant messaging, etc.) has been conceptualized as making the potential content of memories increasingly malleable and ephemeral, related to the discussion of the image in chapter 3 (Murray 2008; Rubenstein and Sluis 2008). Secondly, this is seen as part of a more general shift from practices of preservation and memory-making towards practices of communication in everyday life (van Dijck 2007; Van House and Churchill 2008). As we have seen, José van Dijck (2007) argues that digital is implicated in a gradual shift from the dominance of memory to communication practices in personal photography – or, in other words, that immediacy is taking precedence over archiving, that storing is performed *through* distributing, and that novel ways of classifying and ordering images for the future are emerging as a result. Thirdly, the broader ubiquity of information technology is conceptualized in terms of changing infrastructures of memory, paying detailed attention to how new standards and classifications shape remembering in as yet unforeseen ways (Bowker 2005: 5; also Bowker and Star 1999).

One of the key novelties here is the potentially *endless distribution* of digital photos through databases and web-based platforms implied by the technical architectures examined in chapter 4. While the commodification of photos in social media platforms suggests a more general commodification of memory as a form of exchange, as discussed in chapter 3, there is an *ongoing variation* in the material forms digital photos can take in contrast to print reproduction, suggesting a dynamic of potential openness which has to be *managed* (Van House 2011). The impact of this upon how photos are classified, interpreted and become potential memories seems highly significant, when digital images (whether digital in origin or digitized film prints) can be reworked and recontextualized in ways that seem to be very different from the print album, which at the very least provides a sense of durability. For example, the web-based project www.deadphotographers. co.uk:

> is a forever expanding collection of images which explore the relationship of photography and our changing time while aiming to prove the theory that everyone has a good photograph in them . . . each photograph is collected through house clearances of the deceased, where unwanted items are discarded, including whole photography archives of the once keen photographers.

Such a project of 'resurrection' is made possible by digitization, but makes sense only in tandem with a cultural sensibility that is concerned both with photographic disappearance and with valuing the ordinary and the mundane. In this way the advent of networked information technologies such as the internet tends to encourage remembering rather than forgetting. In tandem with the propensity to recontextualize past moments, another central aspect of this is the way in which the routine use of digital imaging devices and systems, discussed in chapter 4, enables the recording of all but everything in the first place:

> Digital memory, more than any other form of mediation, collapses the assumed distinction between modern 'archival' memory and traditional 'lived' memory by combining the function of storage and ordering on the one hand and of presence and interactivity on the other. (Hoskins 2007: 402)

Most importantly, this is the opposite of what many thought so-called virtual technologies would bring about. For example, it has been argued that the established practices of making memories in modernity are being displaced by more transient and forgettable traces of lived experience in societies characterized by speed (Bauman 2007; Gane 2006; Lash 2002). But, as Latour (2007) has remarked in relation to digitization, in contrast to more traditional memory objects, now seen as vulnerable in digital form, digital traces are *anything but forgettable*, where 'it is as if the inner workings of private worlds have been pried open because their inputs and outputs have become thoroughly traceable'. Often referred to as active and passive 'footprints' of everyday life, the private lives of others are becoming increasingly public in a kind of vast archive (Featherstone 2000; Gane and Beer 2008) shaped partly by corporate interests (Thrift 2005).

This shift towards digital databases and associated systems is precipitating a set of conflicting concerns and responses. On the one hand, digital memory is cheap, such that we *routinely* store vast amounts of digital data and thus appear to remember a great deal, both individually and collectively. On the other hand, new technologies change what can be remembered, and how it can be remembered, with specific consequences for notions of permanence and authentic interpretation. One way of thinking about this is to consider how memories become inscribed in material forms and how those material forms shape the nature of the memory. For example, the development of writing technologies (alphabets, wax tablets, parchments, and so on) enabled stories and conversations to be made concrete and reproduced over time with arguably more stability than with the voice (e.g., religious texts). Most importantly, the written inscription is made stable and so available for continued analysis in that form. Specifically, the different storage, distribution, classification and retrieval possibilities enabled by technologies alter what it is possible to know and remember (e.g., hieroglyphs versus Twitter). This is of particular importance in the sciences, where the ability to record and share data over time and space enables the very idea of verifiable scientific knowledge to exist. As Bowker (2005) observes, the systems in which knowledge is made shape the possibilities of what we can say about the past. As observed in chapter 3, the material form photographs take may alter how they can be interpreted in the future. The inscriptions we find on the back of print images retain their meaning when their context can be understood (i.e., in an album). When we come across old family photos in antique shops or yard sales, it is almost impossible to understand their content or meaning, as they have become separated from their original classification system. So, when images circulate through multiple systems (networked databases), what we can know about them alters.

The combination of networked databases and visual media, for example in social media like Facebook, has arguably made mundane acts of classification and ordering increasingly self-conscious and reflexive as they become visible to others. Some of these involve people deciding what counts as private or public, online and offline, but also the extent to which classification software increasingly intervenes in the structuring of consumption. In this sense, 'Contemporary memory is thoroughly interpenetrated by a technological unconscious in that there occurs a co-evolution of memory and technology. Memory is readily and dynamically configured through our digital practices and the connectivity of our networks' (Hoskins 2009: 96). Changes in the technologies of organization – from the album to the cloud – are highly significant, I suggest, for how we think about individual and collective memory. In line with the argument about practice, we should consider here how personal photographically orientated memory is performed on the ground. We may be producing a great deal more visual content than can be remembered, but the questions remain as to *what it is* and *how* it will be remembered. Have the new modes of classification and memory-making made possible by digital images and infrastructures displaced their analogue counterparts, and with what consequences? How do individuals *manage* their digital photos in relation to issues of preservation and communication?

Family albums, social cohesion

As discussed in chapter 2, the practice of photography has since its inception been intimately bound up with the domestic sphere, within which the modern notions of leisure, family and home have co-evolved with photography (Spence and Holland 1991). The standardization of the family album occurred during the 1860s in Britain through the carte de visite, but we see the real rise of domestic 'family' or personal photography and its invocation of 'happy memories' during the 1950s. Slater (1995) and others have argued that photography is a central feature of Western modernity (in terms of aesthetics and technology) and, following this, that domestic photography was integral to self-conscious identity formation in the twentieth century in particular. Indeed, the primary focus for those who have studied the actual practices of photo-making in everyday life has been the significance of albums and photos for individual identity, belonging and family cohesion (Csikszentmihalyi and Rochberg-Halton 1981; Hirsch 1981; King 1986; Chalfen 1987; Spence and Holland 1991). The particular ordering of photographs, as well as their content, has been instrumental in articulating specific narratives of the family, especially those of chronology, and of the domestic during the late nineteenth and especially the twentieth century – with the production of idealized images of familial life arguably being the most crucial. The ideals of domestic life are often constructed though specific events such as birthdays, weddings and holidays, which have come to structure what counts as 'normal' narratives of familial life. In this sense, private leisure has been the key object of family album-making and the marketing of photographic equipment and potential uses. The connections between photography, childhood, and tourism as articulated in the domestic sphere have also been – and continue to be – central to the expansion of personal photography as a commercial and consumerist activity (Slater 1995).

The production of family albums (rather than photographs per se) can be seen as relatively self-conscious efforts to *produce* memory. The very activity of looking through copious images of oneself and familiar others, either individually or collectively, is a rich act of self-reflection and contemplation (Spence and Holland 1991). It is in this sense also that memory-making can be self-conscious, more or less organized through juxtaposition and ordering, and also reflexively tied to the dominant technologies deployed. As Spence and Holland argued in their definitive collection about album-making, practices of image-making are diverse but also are constrained by the collectively defined conventions of what is pictured and how it is done. Family albums often reproduce somewhat sentimental images of the everyday, and in the process launder some of the more conflictual aspects of domesticity. The values of particular conventions of memory-making are all too evident and have often rendered domestic photography as banal (see Bourdieu 1990a). The notion of banality has in part been reflected in the lack of serious attention paid to the richness of personal domestic photography, with the notable exceptions above. It is rather difficult to access the rich context of particular domestic images retrospectively, especially as the majority of these, though they may reside in the context of whole albums, were never explicitly intended to be publicly viewed. In other words, private images of this kind are not so easily subject to aesthetic criticism or empirical analysis. This is changing as a result of digitization, where ordinary practices of image-making have become pervasive and available.

It was initially thought that, in late modern individualized culture, the family album was anyway undergoing something of a demise in terms of its centrality to identity formation, and would therefore be largely unaffected by digitization (see Slater 1995). For Slater, the 'privatization of leisure' formed the primary context within which the digitization of snapshot photography would most likely be inserted. This refers to the movement of consumer expenditure into the home, as increasing numbers of entertainment commodities are located there – for example, television, video games, hi-fi, and so on. This might now be extended to consider the proliferation of multiple screens (flat screen television, PCs and laptops, hand-held devices) and a novel infrastructure in the form of home Wi-Fi networks for the distribution of data flows throughout the domestic environment. It is in this sense, argues Slater (1995), that we see Williams's (1974) notion of 'mobile privatization' taking real shape – where the privacy of the family home is enacted through *individualized* mobile technologies of one kind or another. More recently, it has been almost universally argued that digital photography has not only moved beyond the collectively produced family album, partly in tandem with this broader phenomenon, but has reshaped the whole process of photographic memory-making from fixing images to *exchanging* them (e.g., Murray 2008; van Dijck 2011; Van House and Churchill 2008). In what follows, I examine several current trends in digital personal photography and memory that are located in or connected to the domestic sphere.

Archive anxiety, shoeboxes and memory sticks

> The world's computers are brimming over with personal treasures of every genre (music, pictures, texts), but no one guarantees the preservation of electronic materials for generations to come. Machines and software formats may become obsolete, hard drives are anything but robust, and digital files may start to degrade or become indecipherable. Ironically, problems of preservation and access to personal memories, as a result of their digital condition, could become even more complex than before. (Van Dijck 2007)

As we have seen, those who use digital cameras often speak anecdotally about the sheer volume of images they have stored, usually on their hard drive, as a consequence of the routine presence of cameras and the cultural expectations of immediate image production. For those images not deleted, people speak of how to go about *organizing* them, how to select specific images for other purposes such as giving gifts or displaying, and are regularly concerned about their potential disappearance. Interestingly, younger people such as university students are now as equally concerned about their unexpected *permanence*.

In the first instance, then, one of the most commonplace and problematic issues for domestically anchored photography is what to do with burgeoning volumes of digital images. There are some clear, practical issues here with which most people will be familiar. For example, is there any reason to make prints of digital images when they can be stored in software-generated or web-based 'albums'? Should I keep all the images I have produced? Should I store my images on multiple formats such as external hard drives, CDs, memory sticks, and so on? While such questions have a somewhat ordinary character, they are folded into issues of memory-making, narrative construction, technological forecasting (which technology and classification system will last *longest*?) and anxieties about potential memory loss. The ways in which people answer these questions through practical engagement are of great significance for what kind of material lives digital images may have. As van Dijck (2007) astutely observes, digital photography is producing different kinds of materiality and performativity, but digital images live alongside traditional modes of display and storage, such as the framed print and the scrapbooked image. In other words, we should not simply assume that the databases of online photo-sharing sites have replaced other modes of collation, ordering and classification, but ask what the relations between them are.

In a broader sense, intimated by van Dijck (2007), these daily decisions being made about storage and distribution on the ground have implications for the autobiographies and potential memories of individuals involved, but also for memory-making on different scales – of nation, region, generation, and so on. The nature of this relationship is presenting archivists with acute problems of how to preserve twenty-first-century artefacts and even of how to decide what to preserve in the first place (Hand 2008). This is nowhere more obvious than in the case of burgeoning numbers of images and the multiple technological systems within which they are stored, duplicated, altered and multiplied, and through which they migrate. Personal photographers face much the same problems:

> Then I got into the process of loading them on the computer and deleting them off the card, right? Well, I deleted them all off the card, and, as I was proceeding . . . this happened at this family thing I was at. I downloaded the card, I erased the card, loaded the next card and my hard drive crashed. So I lost all the ones that I had just deleted off the card. So, now I don't delete anything until I know things are saved. And then I delete the cards. But I don't delete in the camera unless I am very . . . unless I don't care that I lose everything, like I double, triple check that, yes, it's just that one picture that I'm wiping out. (S, receptionist)

> I've got one big problem with digital, and it's a big one. It's the question about archival nature. You could lose everything. These memory cards don't last, hard drives don't last, so what you're faced with in a way is every five years you've got to monitor your hard drive. Every five years you've got to, if you're safe, you've gotta convert. That is a pain in the neck. I think the digital industry, the digital photography industry, they should accept that as a responsibility of theirs. Because otherwise they're selling you . . . it's like me giving you a cheque that I write with disappearing ink. (X, retired)

Aside from anxieties about accidental deletion or irrevocable loss, people often express concern over the inability to organize, classify or even *look* at all their digital images in ways that are meaningful for them (Van House 2011). It is important to note here, though, that there is not necessarily anything new about this. Most photographs are never looked at again, no matter how 'well organized' they are, and it makes little difference whether they are film or digital; as Bowker has observed in relation to the deterministic notion that memory can be definitively organized in advance, 'the act of rendering memorable does not mean that at any stage it will be remembered' (2005: 16). Although one of the main features of digitization is this proliferation or *overproduction* of photos made possible by the storage capacities of the camera-computer, many people used film in similar ways, producing vast collections of negatives and prints which never see the light of day:

> They started in albums. I started taking pictures when I was in grade 6. My grandmother gave me a camera in grade 6. So I have about twenty-five of those . . . you know those magnetic albums, the 100 pages . . . I have about twenty-five of those that go from, you know, when I was grade 6 on. (A, legal secretary)

Perhaps counter-intuitively, what does appear to be different at the level of practice is the heightened possibility of viewing photos on the computer rather than those stored in printed albums. This is partly to do with a perceived ease of retrieval of the digital in contrast to the difficulties of translating what might have been (at the time) entirely rational modes of classification into effective strategies or practices of retrieval in the present:

> But I don't look at those [pictures in envelopes]. I only go through those if I'm looking for something specific, if I have to get pictures from a past event or if I'm doing a photo contest and I think, 'Oh, I took a picture of . . .'. One time . . . I couldn't remember exactly what year it was, so I went back through those boxes to find it. And then took that in and got it reprinted. It's a lot easier to find things now on the computer. (A, legal secretary)

The phenomenon of 'having too many pictures', whether they are film or digital, presents people with dilemmas of organization. For some, digitization has produced this problem in a form that did not previously exist, as the quantitative difference between film and digital for them is stark. For others, organizing photos has always been something of a burden, with digitization *intensifying* this problem to a degree when it has led to an exponential increase in printing:

> Before I had children [laughs] . . . then they got really far
> behind. And then I spent an entire winter, and that's where
> I got to 2004. I spent an entire winter with these because I
> couldn't stand that I couldn't find pictures. Now I've sort of
> fallen into that trap with the digitals that are printed. They're
> not as organized as this yet. No, they're kind of half and half.
> I'm just waiting for that lottery ticket, you know, the one
> that lets me have a holiday and sort through those things. It
> hasn't come yet. (C, nurse)

When the difference between film and digital is enacted
in terms of the printed album and the digitized album, other
issues of classification arise. The differences between traditional and online albums have implications for the processes
of memory-making and for the transformation of circulated
images into 'fixed' ones. As any archivist will tell us, the precise *order* in which an album has been constructed, and the
ways in which particular images are placed in relation to one
another and the album as a whole, form the key to understanding the contextual meaning of any one image rather than
its specific content. A relational view of meaning is preferred
here and raises questions about the implications for memory
when images are *not* stored in this way, or when the original
order of things cannot be retrieved or has been subject to continual reworking in a data stream rather than a fixed album.

Some of the organizational and classification practices
associated with album-making are in fact reproduced in digital photography, sometimes because the software through
which the pictures are stored replicates the conventions of
chronology, but also because some people try to do this more
self-consciously.

> I've stopped writing on the back of them because I've heard
> that degenerates the quality, but, yeah, a little piece of paper
> you slip into the albums where you write where you went and
> any comments, what building it was and dates and things
> like that. Not in too much detail, but enough detail to sort of
> spark my memory. (M, retail assistant)

Most cameras and PCs, laptops and other devices, come with pre-loaded software that in most cases automatically classifies and orders downloaded photos (usually in date order, but also going by events, places and faces). Anecdotally it seems that most people do 'not get around' to reclassifying their photos by description, annotation, theme, a non-linear classification, and so on (Van House 2011). For some individuals, there are now different modes of classification operating in different systems – camera, PC, memory stick, online repository – which creates difficulties of retrieval and memory:

> I don't get into this automated software stuff that people put out for this. I just find it way too complicated for me. So I think I am definitely organized on the computer. I'm not so organized with the disks that I've made as a backup. I don't have a filing system for them. You know what I mean? I have to go through all those disks to find where are those zoo shots? Cause I can't even tell you how I've labelled them. I'm hoping I've labelled them properly, but I have no idea. So I have to put those in the computer, look at them, see what they are and then label them. So that's where my organization falls off, but clearly now I have a need to do it because I have had a crash and I want to reload. I want my dragonfly pictures back and I don't know where they are. (S, administrator)

Others have adopted software specifically designed to address issues of organization, memory and retrieval – for example, prompting users to back up their images: 'It's software I bought through Creative Memories. So it pops up every once in a while, you know. You haven't backed up and there's 364 new pictures to back up' (M, homemaker).

While for some people the default settings (e.g., date order) of the software are unproblematic, for others there are novel problems of classification opened up by the apparent possibilities afforded by *multiple* folders and *inexhaustible* ways of sorting and developing new categories that have become a burden in their own right:

> Well, for a while I was putting them under a heading, just a random ... I was putting them under the wrong heading. We used to have a car for sale. I was putting everything under there, but then I learned that you can have a generic folder, and then from there I divide the images up. If there's, say, pictures of the house and pictures of the cat or something. So I divide it from the generic folder, and this folder is kept empty and I think it's just called something like um ... pictures or something, and then the other folders have actual names of places. (F, homemaker)

Another important aspect here is how people see their digital images individually rather than as part of a collection. Each image tends to be viewed individually on the screen rather than collectively on an album page:

> Actually um ... when I'm putting stuff in albums I'm much more visually aware of the layout, I think. I tend to ... it tends to be chronological to an extent, and but it also tends to be ... if I have lots of pictures of one area, I'll try to get all the nature pictures together and all the church pictures together, so group the pictures like that, to an extent. Whereas on the computer it just tends to be a random ... well, it's not a random strip of images ... but I'm not so aware of that because you tend to look at pictures individually. I think that's why. (F, homemaker)

The coupling of the camera with computer and network capabilities is enabling novel modes of sharing and exchange to emerge and take hold. This might involve the use of the laptop to view photos collectively, remediating earlier practices of flicking through the print album (Shove et al. 2007). This can also be extended across time and space, opening up the family album to friends and relatives who are not physically present but connected via information networks and screens, performing the kind of 'distant closeness' (Van House 2007) associated with social networking. Visual accounts of events can be shared and viewed immediately after they have taken place, rather than having to be viewed in the printed album at a later stage. To reiterate the critique of any notion of seamless interoperability here, the simple sharing of images via email relies, of course, on people having similar equipment, knowledge and skill.

> I think because my family's in England, my husband's family's in Calgary. So we don't have many people to show them to . . . so it's just mostly us two looking at them, and we have them all vaguely catalogued on the internet . . . I mean on the computer. So we've sent them to people, but we've never needed to really print any of them. We did do a little, like about four or five to send to his family. Roy's family we have to do hard copies because they're not computer literate . . . that's why we printed his graduation. (S, stage manager)

> So what I do is, the family pictures that I take, because my family is big on reunions and get-togethers, right? So I sit there with my camera and take the pictures, then I put them on a disk and I throw them all out to them and say, 'You print what you like'. So I print a small sample of things from family stuff and I take them in the album when I go. So, and I also have elderly parents, and my mother can't do the digital thing because they go by too fast, so I print off some stuff for her because she likes to look at hard copies. But she likes the instant thing too, where you can just print them off and show them to her. She doesn't have to wait for them to come back from the store and all that stuff. (T, administrator)

As I showed in chapter 4, in contrast to the simple analogue to digital narrative, the increased range of digital and non-digital technologies and systems that can be interconnected produces a tremendous variety of possible trajectories for actual practice. In the above, we have seen different combinations of devices, systems and classificatory conventions and schemes employed for locally specific reasons. Each of these in turn enables and constrains the possibilities for photo storage, distribution, exchange and retrieval in ways that are reconfiguring the album.

Reconfiguring the album
Some of the accounts above also speak to how the 'responsibilities' for organization, classification and memory have

Figure 5.1   Scrapbooking

altered (or not) in the domestic context. As discussed in chapters 2 and 4, for most of the twentieth century the production
of photos in the domestic sphere was undertaken mainly by
men, with the collation and storage done by women. The
individualization of image-making technologies has problematized traditional memory-making roles in the domestic
context. Initially, many early adopters of consumer-orientated
digital cameras in the late 1990s were males in white-collar
professions. As the camera was often positioned as an ally
of the home computer, which had itself been positioned as a
'masculine' technology, there was a temporary shift in image-
storing expertise to the male of the household. The traditional
album-making activities of the housewife shifted to the work-
orientated use of the personal computer. As general computer
skills have proliferated, as part of the broadening of access and
reconfiguration of 'digital divides' (from patterns of access to
patterns of use), what appears to be happening now is the proliferation of *individual archives* in the domestic environment,
with each member of the household constructing their own

versions of that domestically anchored memory (Shove et al. 2007; van Dijck 2007; Van House 2011).

What is significant about this? First, this is the outcome of the use of cameras by children and teenagers – the result of the free and disposable nature of digital images such that parents allow children to use the camera or have individual cameras in ways previously prohibited by the cost of film and the expectation that there would be only one camera per household. The shift in uses here has, in turn, been observed by manufacturers, which now market cameras to child consumers. Secondly, and more specifically, it suggests the potential for the *democratization* of domestic memory-making and of how, in practice, family members will differentiate between multiple representations of the 'same' family or household. As such, we are witnessing a *multiplication* of album-making rather than its disappearance.

In the discussion above, it is largely assumed that the majority of digital images exist online or in some other digital form. But since around 2005 there has also been a notable rise in the printing of these images, partly as a response to issues of 'digital decay', but also in conjunction with those other presumptive technologies of visual culture such as card-making and scrapbooking (see www.creativememories.com). In North America, one of the most popular contexts for the popularity of digital photography is scrapbooking. This has become a major industry, involving a large retail sector, formal and informal associations, individual practices, and so on, which exemplify a number of important issues.

To begin, the practice of scrapbooking *integrates* digital cameras, memory sticks, computers, and printing technologies into a relatively coherent configuration. It is a specific performance of these materials that relies upon and produces new demand for high-quality printers and paper. Print persists here, and in many ways this is a key contemporary form of the necessarily *intertextual* nature of photography since its inception as a modern practice (Lister 1995).

> I mean, scrapbooking is sort of . . . well . . . it's like recording events and journalling about it and things like that. I have in some way always done that because I've always written on the back of the photos, and in those old magnetic photos I've always taken stickies and written the date and some little thing about it . . . It's just more evolved than that now . . . Actually, I've done about twenty-five albums, but they've all been gifts almost. (A, legal secretary)

It follows that, as an overwhelmingly female pursuit, scrapbooking is an extension and variation of compiling the modern family album, reproducing the gendered responsibilities of order and collation, while increasing the parameters of what can be scrapbooked and how this might be annotated through 'journalling':

> Well, that's one of the things that they really encourage, at least with this particular company – this *Creative Memories* – is the journalling to make sure you write it down. Their goal is that you, a perfect stranger, could sit there on your own and still get a sense of the story behind the pictures. (M, homemaker)

In other words, digitization allows for a *reinvigoration* or 'remediation' (Bolter and Grusin 1999) of what is essentially a form of album-making, which can co-exist with other forms of digital memory making. Finally, scrapbooking is precisely the kind of practice illuminated by Campbell's (2005) notion of 'craft consumption', mentioned in chapters 2 and 4, whereby consumers purchase materials in order to construct their own commodities.

In this particular context, digital photography is enabling a reconfiguration of album-making, incorporating many traditional aspects of that practice, including linear narratives of family memory and fixed forms of classification, as digital images are embedded in the print formation of the contemporary scrapbook. At the same time, scrapbooking and related craft activities are providing another context through which photography is given new life. The often restricted academic focus upon how digitization enables novel photo-blogs, for example, needs to be tempered with recognition of the *simultaneous* rise of craft-orientated digital practices of memory-making.

The ways in which people deal with the substantively greater numbers of images they produce are immensely varied. There are several emerging trajectories here, with new technologies enabling the co-existence of multiple modes of memory-making, storage and classification, which in isolation raise important questions about retrieval but in combination present us with a somewhat bewildering landscape of inter-connected practices. While the above discussion focuses primarily upon practices within the domestic sphere, and that to some extent remain private, there has been a more radical series of developments in image distribution that arguably transform the very meaning of public and private memory.

Distribution: sharing photos and the politics of tagging

> The idea of 'in the past' is in the past. Impossible to put aside childish things because Google knows where they are; and even if you take them down, the Wayback Machine will cache them for all time. So that's that for the past. (Bywater 2010)

If the emergence of parallel personal archives – where many or all members of a household are storing photographic images on a large scale – represents a horizontalization of domestic photographic memory, further complexities arise when we consider the advent and prevalence of new web-based forms of image organization, ordering and distribution. As discussed earlier, much is being made of the notion that the private lives of others are becoming increasingly public, as they are often voluntarily made visible and retrievable through the uploading of personal photographic images to online environments such as Flickr and Facebook. As practices of making, storing and distributing photographic images are privatized and to some extent individualized, the images produced have become at the same time more publicly accessible and collectively defined and organized than ever before. While digital photography has many diverse trajectories and material forms, as above (photojournalling, scrapbooking, etc.), the specific enfolding of digital image-making, storage and distribution with social networking is having significant and more pervasive transformative impacts upon people's actual engagement with and conceptualization of photographic practices (see also Van House 2011).

In particular, this is producing novel aspects to how photos are contextualized and recontextualized, classified and reclassified. The use of information technologies to distribute photos to known others (relatives, friends) can be radically extended here in the form of an opening up of images to potentially limitless others in social media platforms. The naming and potential renaming of specific images through individual and collective processes of tagging and commenting is a substantially novel development when seen in terms of the relationships between individual and group memory. I want to concentrate here specifically on the practices of tagging and commenting, as they signal both an expansion of who is deemed *responsible* for memory-making and the intimation of anxieties about the nature of digital photographic traces in wider flows of information.

Flickr, Facebook and the tagged visual landscape
In chapters 2 and 4, I discussed some of the dynamics of pervasive information networks and how some scholars in cultural sociology and geography have argued that new *materialities of information* are emerging, from geolocational systems to increasingly dense and yet invisible layers of software operating in the urban fabric. One aspect of this, examined in chapter 4, is the rise of so-called prosumptive technologies and practices that, to some extent, rely upon the digitally mediated intersection of production and consumption. If there was,

and perhaps still is, a commonly cited feature of the 'semantic web', it is the practice of content generation by users through sites such as YouTube (Burgess and Green 2009), Facebook, Flickr, and a variety of participatory media (Jenkins 2006) which purport to have democratized cultural production and to have empowered individuals to become full prosumers of cultural artefacts (cf. Beer 2009; Beer and Burrows 2007; Keen 2007; Leadbeater 2008; O'Reilly 2005). Within this consensual narrative of Web 2.0 emerging in the mid-2000s, it is defined as a 'second upgraded version of the web that is more open, collaborative, and participatory' (O'Reilly 2005). According to Lenhardt and Madden (2005), the applications of Web 2.0 have become 'an embedded and routine part of contemporary everyday life, particularly for young people'. Beer and Burrows (2007) explain that the applications such as MSN, Facebook, Flickr, blogger, and YouTube are:

> dynamic matrices of information through which people observe others, expand the network, make new 'friends', edit and update content, blog, remix, post, respond, share files, exhibit, tag and so on . . . where users are increasingly involved in creating web content as well as consuming it.

It is important to recognize that these accounts are usually conjoined with notions of a generational shift, wherein the aforementioned reproduction of analogue album-making practices is confined largely to those over the age of thirty. Various terminologies are used here for the under thirties, from specifying the differences between 'digital immigrants' and 'digital natives', to the more general notion of Generation C – those who both produce and manipulate cultural content through the consumption of digital devices and technologies of storage, display and distribution. The point of this in the context of this chapter is that this generation (if we can call it that) engages in the practices *as a matter of routine* rather than as isolated incidents of reflexive engagement.

In the language of cultural theory, those who are engaging

with participatory media are facilitating a culture that emerges through perpetual acts of *performative transmission* rather than through methods of more considered representation. For some, this has had a profound effect on the nature of individual photos:

> Within online networks the individual snapshot is stripped of the fragile aura of the photographic object as it becomes absorbed in a stream of visual data. By giving up the attributes of a photograph as a unique, singular and intentional presence, the networked snapshot is becoming difficult to comprehend with the conceptual tools of visual literacy and photographic theory. (Rubenstein and Sluis 2008: 23)

This idea – that a networked or shared photo is stripped of intentionality – would seem particularly significant when we think of how convergences of digital photography and social media are being enacted in relation to memory. As Van House et al. (2005) have shown, sharing photos is of course facilitated through the synchronicity of cameras and social media, but there are a variety of ways in which users choose to share or not share photos, to classify and organize them, related to issues of memory, expression, representation and relationship management. The popular impression of photo tagging – the assigning of a keyword to the image, or the digital annotation of images – is one of a habitual and unreflexive mode of ordering, as opposed to the more considered management of what photos to post in which social networking site. As Van House (2007) has shown, many younger people assume that tagging is just 'what you are supposed to do', but are quite careful about constructing photo profiles for different audiences.

It is worth reiterating here the sheer scale of uploaded photos in photo-sharing databases to signal the significance of tagging and commenting as modes of classification. One billion photos are uploaded to Facebook each month. There are 250 million users, 120 million of which log on to use Facebook each day. In the case of the photo-sharing site Flickr, there

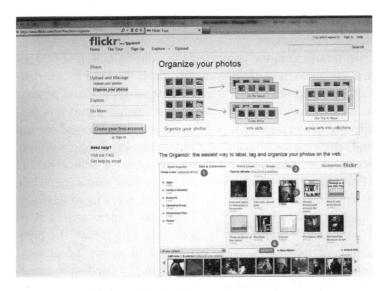

Figure 5.2   Flickr classifications

are approximately 5,000 uploads per minute, several million images geotagged per month, and hundreds of thousands of collaboratively tagged images under the most popular tags. Tagging of this kind involves the addition of keywords to images, resulting in a bottom-up form of categorization. This might be used to classify a personal set of images and also to make those images searchable within photo-sharing websites. As Rubinstein and Sluis (2008) observe, 'Tagging, commenting, titling and annotating of images are essential elements of participation in the social aspects of photo-sharing which play a role in creating communities of users interested in specific images' (2008: 19).

This is certainly the case with Flickr, which has been the most commonly researched site for an emerging scholarly literature about photo-sharing and processes of tagging (e.g., van Dijck 2011; Van House 2011). There are several important insights from this research that are important in their own right and which also provide a starting point for developing a more focused examination of tagging and commenting practices in Facebook.

In returning to the context of the overproduction of images and the problem of archive anxiety, those working in information science and archival science have conceptualized tagging as an immanent 'solution' to these problems. From this perspective, photo tagging is positioned as a useful way of sorting and retrieving the blizzard of images stored and shared online. Its assumed purposes for users are ones of self-conscious efforts to organize and order this new visual landscape, while at the same time recognizing the subtle ways in which such ordering remembers some things and forgets others (Van House and Churchill 2008). Within this literature, the prevalence of tagging is often expressed in subtly teleological form – that users and perhaps photography itself were somehow waiting for better sharing architectures to emerge.

The practice of tagging is often referred to as 'social tagging' when it is collectively orientated, not necessarily intentionally but as an outcome of the process. In this sense, a horizontalization or democratization of image ordering and potential memory occurs: 'Tagging subverts any attempt to impose narrative order on the snapshot collection, and calls into question a snapshot's specificity or individual mark of identity. As a process it acts to join images together as communal pools of tourist maps, sunsets and babies' (Rubenstein and Sluis 2008: 19).

In a site like Flickr, the interest has been on the ways in which user-generated content is tagged by users and generates 'clouds of tags', sometimes described as Folksonomies. Flickr then tracks the popularity of specific tags in order to create new suggestive categories for photo searching, such as 'most interesting'. While Flickr represents the kind of site where images are central, in many ways it is the textual traces here that are significant, I think, but more important than that are the ways in which tags are *read by other software* to create new classifications.

A key observation arising from this is that online photo-sharing and tagging has reconfigured the purpose and practice of photography to a great extent – de-centring the visual *content* of photos and emphasizing their communicative value, as indicated by van Dijck (2011) and others. In other words, there has been a shift from images being 'talked about' to images in some sense 'doing the talking'. Lerman and Jones (2006) refer to this as 'social browsing', where users browse the latest photos of their listed contacts in order to follow the narratives of their everyday lives. Similarly, images are increasingly being used dialogically, particularly where previously marginal mundane objects now populate Flickr alongside more conventional aesthetic forms, promoting a 'Flickr aesthetic'. In this sense, they become the means for a form of communication that is ongoing and potentially democratic between disparate and unknown individuals organized via tag clouds (Murray 2008).

Drawing again upon the notion of redistributed agency in sociotechnical systems, it can be argued that photo-sharing is not so much about people intentionally and self-consciously sharing images as it is about technologies or devices distributing images between themselves via software as it 'sinks' into ordinary practice. Of considerable importance here is the preloading and black boxing of metadata-tagging functions in cameraphones and digital cameras, as we saw in chapter 4, plus the real-time uploading facilities of cameras and smartphones. The key aspect of this is the largely invisible performativity or agency of metadata – the data that organize and channel flows of information (as in tagging). Metadata provide:

> a means for the image to escape its original context. Stripped of their interfaces, photo-sharing sites function as vast databases of indexed photographs which can be remixed and remapped online as mashups . . . these practices illustrate the way in which the networked image is data, that is: visual information to be analyzed and remapped to new contexts via algorithms. (Rubenstein and Sluis 2008: 21–2)

As van Dijck (2011: 2) notes: 'the idea of "sharing" presumes a conscious, human activity, whereas in the context of social media platforms it has become mostly an unconscious technological pursuit.' This is related to the broader conceptualization of contemporary cultures of information, where:

> The shift . . . is toward information becoming a part of how we live, a part of our being, a part of how we do things, the way we are treated, the things we encounter, our way of life. The result is that information is not only about how we understand the world, it is also active in constructing it. (Beer 2009; see also Dodge and Kitchen 2008)

Thrift (2005) describes this as the 'technological subconscious' – the ways in which invisible software machines are increasingly producing and organizing everyday life (see also Elliot and Urry 2010). Similarly, N. Katherine Hayles says that these developments have the 'power to affect cultural formations' (in Gane et al. 2007). The level and scale of computation in the environment again raises questions about human and non-human agency within 'performative infrastructures' (Thrift 2005: 224), where metadata (such as data involved in tagging) *act* to direct, channel, block and allow flows of information, which in this case are the mechanisms of classification and potential memory (see Lash 2007).

As suggested by the research above, the specificity of particular images in photo-sharing platforms is an outcome of the context or interface of their consumption, rather than their meaning in any traditional or, indeed, modern sense of representation. But, as an initial critique, metadata and tagging are assumed here to have the same ordering or folksonomic effects across social media platforms, which may be rather different in a number of ways. By focusing upon Facebook rather than Flickr, I want to show how photo tagging might be a rather different practice in relation to different social media and the ways in which they are embedded in and augment different forms of social networking and memory practices. The use of images in Facebook profiles at first glance appears to have more in common with conventional album-making – in that it is not quite the public sharing architecture that Flickr is, and photos are often organized into albums in far more conventional ways than in Flickr. The most significant difference here is that tagging in a site like Flickr involves using a tag to describe the image, whereas in Facebook it is used primarily to name individuals within images. In Facebook, the practice of tagging *individuals* in an image opens the albums of others (to whom one may have no relationship or tie) for social browsing. While academic interest in Facebook has waned somewhat (but see Miller 2011) in tandem with its ubiquity, I find its prevalence interesting and important to explore in terms of emerging relations between individual and collective memory on a significant scale.

The main focus developed here is that, as software is increasingly sinking in to ordinary memory practices – in this case, of photo-sharing – novel *ethical* questions arise as aspects of photographic practice and ordinary life are made visible and require explicit ethical attention and judgement, especially in terms of potential and actual memories.

Tagging and commenting in practice
There is little ethnographic or sustained qualitative research specifically on photo tagging and commenting that draws upon the accounts of users themselves. So in this section I will continue to complement the literature discussed by selectively drawing upon extensive interview and observational data, in this case with undergraduate students, in order to explore the increasing distribution of digital images through photo-sharing and social networking sites. I address the implications of photographic engagement, classification, and memory when images appear always in transmission and re-enactment within these affective environments. For example, how do people actually negotiate practices of digital image-making, storage, and distribution online? How are emotional attachments to personal digital images interpreted

and managed in the quasi-public space of Facebook? What are the emerging relationships between images, software, and the processes of photo tagging, de-tagging and commenting?

The vast majority of undergraduate students in North America, Northern Europe, Japan, and other advanced capitalist societies are using web-based media for the storage, distribution and manipulation of their digital images. With minimal exceptions, having a public profile is a necessity for today's student. Most have a profile on Facebook, largely because of the fact that access to information about events and pictures from those events are only available to those with a Facebook account. Public profiles are often seen to be as essential as cellphones and email – peers simply expect it (see Baym 2010). When asked about their photographic practices, students talk about how they assemble the components of photo-making, storage and sharing, how they use or do not use elements of the software and social media, how they see their relationships with images, and how social relations are mediated through their images. Although students such as these exemplify the 'digital generation', many talk about how particular conventions of image-making and distribution in relation to memory inherited from their parents may or may not 'stick' despite the changing media landscape. For example, the students all presented detailed ways of organizing and making sense of their photos. Not all photos had the same value, and, significantly, nor did they all share the same fate. Some photographs were stored without much thought onto CDs, DVDs, memory sticks or external hard drives; others were instantly shared on Facebook or blogs and through email. 'Special' moments were often kept in additional folders and/ or printed and displayed in frames, albums or scrapbooks, and some photographs were only seen by a very select number of people, namely relationship partners. In other words, even at the individual level we find a multiplicity of photo memory practices embodying different classification schemes and cultural values of durability *and* ephemerality.

The majority of students expressed degrees of anxiety, concern and fascination with the visual landscapes encountered through Facebook. It should be recognized that there may be very different reasons for joining social networking sites. For example, L and D were both 'pressured' into creating a Facebook account. D's account was actually set up for her by the same friend who 'made D join a Facebook' group, which filled her email with notices from Facebook. But a number of consistent themes emerge here – about ownership as a mode of classification, about viewing the photo streams of others, and about the sheer numbers being uploaded. For example, the vast number of photographs on Facebook was a source of both bewilderment and critique:

> Like, you go through a a hundred different photos of the same person smiling with different people, but doing the exact same thing. Like, why? What is the purpose of that kind of photo is what I'm wondering. I mean, is it just like . . . like somebody's kind of vanity, or is it just to say, like, they were here? (A, student)

> People who put up, like, 300 photos and expect everyone to look through them – it's ridiculous. Who has time for that? (L, student)

> It's just like this alternate universe that I don't want to be a part of . . . It's like this fake surreal way of making relationships, but they're always backed up by the fact, like, oh, I just want to see people's photos – like, I just need to see what they're doing. (H, student)

H added, 'The people that tend to take pictures of other people tend to be keen on sharing them. It's like a status thing, like a popularity contest.' Many of these general comments were about the sheer numbers of images uploaded and the uncertainty of how to interpret this in terms of how meaning could be attributed to them. Other more specific concerns related to the movement and potential circulation of these images beyond the control of the maker:

> Facebook, I think, is too networked for me. There's too much
> possibility for information to come across . . . I see Facebook
> as a really great way to connect and make sure that I've got
> everyone's email address correct and telephone numbers
> correct, and I think it's a good way to send people notes back
> and forth. But I don't buy into the piles of photos and the
> piles of videos. (J, student)

While many are posting images on Flickr as well, very few
students are also engaged in the more prosumptive forms of
blogging or producing and maintaining their own websites.
Some had posted 'really photographic' images on Flickr at
one point or another for purposeful artistic feedback. In most
cases, though, participation was irregular, and most respondents said they had not posted anything for some time. J and
A both had their own websites, but mostly for commercial
purposes: J to communicate with her jewellery customers and
A to advertise his work in photojournalism. With respect to
Facebook and the construction of photo albums, narrative
streams and the self-representation of profiles, several significant issues have emerged concerned with tagging, ownership
and the demands for a public online profile while keeping
'personal' memories 'private'. These issues shed light on
the how conjunctions of images, algorithmic software and
memory practices are producing novel ethical dilemmas.

Practices of photo-sharing
The vast numbers of photos in Facebook, and the organization of the site around the conjunction of individual profiles
with chronological 'news feeds' documenting the lives of
'friends', make this a significant technology of potential
memories. These memories can be considered in terms of
the self-conscious management of profiles by individuals,
the collective generation of profiles, photo streams and feeds
produced through the networked interface, and the unintended life of profiles as viewed by others. For example, it is
well known that employers review the Facebook profiles of

potential employees, as do university administrations (tracking problems such as unauthorized events), not to mention the fact that Facebook is a business, and that business is to sell consumer profiles to marketing firms (Trottier 2010).

Practices of photo-sharing on Facebook can be discussed in terms of three key processes: tagging, de-tagging and commenting; image selection; and image-making. Each of these processes involves modes of classification and implications for potential photo-orientated memories. Although these are inextricably related, it makes sense to examine them in what appears to be reverse chronological order (working back to the image-making process), because what is most significant is how issues arising from tagging processes are generating a sense of uncertainty about how best to make images and select images for posting and sharing.

The near ubiquitous presence of image-capture devices at social events has a direct bearing upon practices of tagging and commenting. After social events, or even during them, tagging and de-tagging operate as modes of owning and disowning images. With the proliferation of digital cameras, someone is always there to capture the event in ways that are far less manageable than in the past. There is unlikely to be a considered request to take a photo, and accordingly individuals are aware of the possibility of being captured in embarrassing situations or having unflattering pictures posted of them on the Web. The 'right' to place a tag on a particular photograph in the first instance belonged to the photographer, but most students report that, in the end, they have little control over what images of them ended up on Facebook. The most that they could do was to ask for the picture to be removed or to 'un-tag' themselves, a process which has the effect of both removing the name on the photo and the photo itself from the profile of the tagged individual and the news feeds of their 'friends'. This has to be done almost immediately if the unwanted circulation of the photo is to be effectively managed. J, for instance, said he was not tagged in any photographs. He explained that he removed *any* tagged images and refuses to tag anyone in his photos: 'I'm sure there are lots of pictures of me out there. But my thing is that I don't want people to be able to see a picture, click on it and go to my profile. That kind of creeps me out.'

The use of tagging as a mode of inserting oneself in and removing oneself from images and of managing the mobility of images speaks to one of the most novel aspects of photo-sharing in Facebook. If one of your 'friends' is tagged in a photo, that photo appears in your news feed. By clicking on it, you are able to access the entire photo stream of which it is part, even if the 'owner' of that stream is not known to you. If there was a print album equivalent of this, it would be asking a complete stranger if you might leaf through their photo albums simply because you have a mutual acquaintance. In this instance, tagging produces a scenario in which one can have unprecedented access to the visual lives of unknown others. This exemplifies how ordinary life has become visual content, and in some cases public to an unprecedented degree. In terms of tagging and de-tagging, it demonstrates the ethical terrain within which these processes of image management and memory work have become so significant.

The experience of L, who said that there are more pictures of her tagged on other people's pages on Facebook than she has posted of herself, also illustrates the ways in which photos circulate via tagging. For L, tagging is a means through which to *distribute* the images to the other people in the photograph. Others, such as C, concerned with maintaining a sense of ownership over the photos and the ability to manage the stream as a kind of *narrative*, said they did not tag people in their photographs 'So you actually have to go into my site and click on that file before you could see yourself', she explained.

Overall, tagging emerges here as a novel mode of multifaceted management, memory work and surveillance for respondents. Photos that they had not even known had been taken suddenly appeared in their list of tagged images. In this

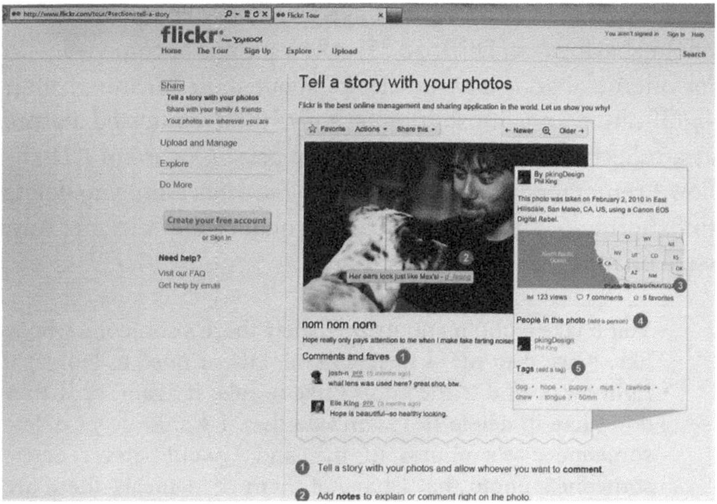

Figure 5.3   Flickr tagging and commenting

way, tagging is not necessarily viewed in a positive light, or in the sense of its being a neutral and useful organizational tool, because respondents' profile images were clearly not entirely under their control. By posting an image of someone and tagging them in it, the 'tagger' asserts ownership over that image and the others in it. This seems especially significant in a visual environment in which, for these students, self-images have strong connections with concerns over self-perception and their social identity:

> I guess we are very vain and self-obsessed sometimes, and we put a lot of meaning in photographs ... such that they really kind of have this kind of fundamental impact on our consciousness and our sense of identity. I guess when people see photos of themselves that aren't too flattering, we tend to react poorly to them, negatively, rather than just brush them off. (A, student)

Some of these issues are resolved or exacerbated by the ability to make comments in a thread attached to images. These are most commonly a central aspect of the dialogic nature of photo-sharing (van Dijck 2007) – how photos become vehicles for often elaborate conversations about their meaning, their significance and, most interestingly, their contested nature as a reflection or representation of a person or event ('That's how I remember this'). At times the requests simply to delete unflattering pictures, rather than to qualify them in this way, were unappreciated or ignored:

> You'll take a photo and immediately there's someone who's, like, 'Give it to me, I need to see'. Like, I need to look at it right away, and if they don't like it, take it again, or if they don't like it, delete it. I won't do that. I would never delete someone else's photos of me, and I would never delete someone's photo that I have of them . . . I mean, there are unflattering photos of everybody. It's not like that's what you really look like. It's not the end of the world. (H, student)

The ever more elaborate personal archive is an unexpected turn enabled primarily because of digital photography. Respondents were mixed on what to do with the multiple versions and accounts of events circulating around them, all of which are contributing to the collective construction of individual memory. While it added to their own archive of images, it also presented a new (and often daunting) task of *constantly monitoring their own public image*, or, in other words, of reflexively engaging with potential memories in the present. In addition, it seems that, while burdened by others' constant concern over self-image, none of the students quite managed to escape it either.

Students were not only more cautious about what images were tagged and therefore linked to their public profiles, but had also become more *selective* in the first instance in the images that they posted of themselves and of others. Van House (2009, 2011) has documented how young people are intensely focused upon calibrating online photos to suit specific audiences. For the students here, this concern has been intensified by the possibilities of future mobility beyond their control. The fact that anyone and everyone can access Facebook was in some ways a deterrent to posting negative images of others, as the act could easily be returned in a kind of online 'war of images'. In other words, it is possible to identify a heightened reflexivity about what to post – a consideration of this in light of potential unintended consequences, as the specific image might be tagged and therefore recontextualized in a way beyond one's control.

Most interestingly, this also extends to the consideration of others in one's own images. For example, C said that, while she enjoys posting photos from her travels, she is careful about what images she selects for uploading. Usually she actually checks with the people in the photograph to see that they do not mind the image being posted. She added that, overall, she does not post much on her Facebook account, because 'Everyone in my class can access that file, and I don't really want to be seen by too many people.'

In this sense, the respondents in many ways had become their own public relations managers. In some ways the proliferation of cameras and the possibilities of online distribution have taught respondents to be more *critical* of images and their ability to represent their subjects 'accurately'. This turned out to be a strange mixture of 'vanity', as A called it, with a considerable awareness of the subjective or arbitrary nature of the camera. Respondents made numerous mentions of having friends who would refuse to have a bad picture of them taken, anticipating the 'hard work' that would then be required to manage their own Facebook profiles and the types of images circulating of them.

> Well, like there are some people that I have on Facebook that are from camp, so they're younger. Like. I have 'Emma' on Facebook who's, like, ten. I have her siblings on Facebook, and, like, there are some pictures there that I don't really want her to see. Not because I'm, like, drinking or anything like that, cause I don't put those kinds of pictures up. I don't

think that's a good way to represent myself and like who I am. (D, student)

H added that, since she does not have a Facebook page, her friends should not feel concerned that she would post them online. However, this does not seem to deter them from *demanding* that the photos be deleted. As H said, 'After a while it gets frustrating. It's like you look that way at the moment – big deal, everyone has their odd moments.' Despite her relaxed attitude, part of H's reasoning for not getting a Facebook account was the stress of having constantly to monitor her profile. Having unflattering images was fine, so long as they stayed in her personal archive.

If concerns about potential tagging practices were collapsing in on issues of which images to upload, this, in turn, seems to work further backwards into considerations of what image to make in the first instance, as we saw in chapter 3. In this way, Facebook and other social media have the dual roles of enabling digital photography to become and remain so pervasive and in reconfiguring many elements of it that extend well beyond these interfaces.

The practice of photo-sharing in Facebook has its own specific dynamics, particularly how the often rather mundane modes of classification, such as simply naming individuals by tagging, seem to have significant unintended consequences when examined in the contexts of photo management and memory practices. The enfolding of digital photography into the dynamic interfaces of social networking sites is making the connections between personal and collective memory and the routine activities of daily life visible and explicit in the sense that it then *requires* intervention and management.

Concluding remarks

In this chapter I have shown that, at the level of ordinary practice, we are indeed seeing the emergence of novel ways of ordering, classifying and distributing digital photos, each of which raises pressing issues for the future of digital memory. I have also stressed the enfolding into these of previous forms of memory work, showing how older practices of album-making and display have remained intact – either quite literally, or in terms of the cultural conventions of photographic order and the salience of recording appropriate life-course moments. We have also seen that, in contrast to the 'from–to' story of digitization, we are seeing a *multiplication* of the materials of memory-making, whether the parallel visual documentation among family members or the simultaneous printing, storing and distribution of the 'same' images for different purposes.

I want to stress the point about the *ongoing* performativity of online photo-sharing. The ways in which ethical notions (such as how to represent others or whether and in what ways one should view and intervene in the visual lives of others) are weaved into and shape these practices are potentially varied, complex and resolutely 'on the move', given the diversity of digital photographic practices in contemporary culture. While many commentators point to the largely invisible impact that software (and the design decisions made about it) has upon everyday life via the 'technological unconscious', the *visualization* or *explicitation* of these questions through the interface is of particular interest in relation to the management of profiles and therefore potential memories. There are new skills (of digital footprint management) emerging in relation to this, alongside a series of unintended consequences of photo-sharing – especially practices of *anticipating* the consequences for the lives of others. The emergent problem of 'how to live publicly' in a post-privacy world is not only about the management of digital self-presentation but also necessarily recognizes the collective nature of digital public life.

Although this chapter has concerned practices of memory-making, it should be reiterated that digital photography is not necessarily primarily *about* making memories. Mediated memories may form one of the key outcomes of doing photography, but that does not mean that this is why people do it; people do not usually consider that this is what they are doing, and, even if they do, this doesn't straightforwardly *make* memories. A more nuanced way of saying this is that memory-making is but one potential aspect of intersecting practices – of friendship maintenance, of gift giving, of habitual snapshot capturing, of communication, and so forth. As van Dijck (2011: 2) says: 'Individuals articulate their identities as social beings by uploading photographs to document their lives; they appear to become part of a social community through photographic exchange and this, in turn, shapes how they watch the world.' In other words, taking digital photos and engaging in continual efforts to manage them both represents an effort to organize the present moment and has the effect of leaving a set of traces. In this sense, the tensions involved in managing digital photos tells us as much about people's sense of anxiety about the present moment – particularly their public visibility – as it does about any desire to remember things.

While individuals are maintaining many versions of their photographic selves for these different purposes (memory, communication, gifts, relationships), it is worth reflecting upon the somewhat anti-archival processes occurring in online social media. There are clear tensions between the circulation and seemingly infinite variation of specific images – this has consequences for the nature of the record, the document, and for collective memory as institutionally understood (Hand 2008). It remains to be seen whether and in what ways individual biographies continue to be articulated *along many lines* (some of which operate in tag clouds, some of which are materialized in the print album) within a multiplication of possible technological forms.

CHAPTER SIX

Conclusion: Ubiquitous Photography and Public Culture

In this concluding chapter I use the key debates throughout the book to reflect upon several important implications stemming from the ubiquity of photography. I have drawn upon the available research alongside some original empirical material in order to show how digitization has encouraged both an unprecedented proliferation of image-making and distribution and a radical diversification and specialization of what counts as photography in contemporary culture. Photography now has many *co-existent* lives, each of which is part of a different trend and may have a very different trajectory in the future, but all have significant connections with earlier photographies. The nature of some connections continues almost seamlessly after digitization, where well-established conventions of aesthetics are enfolded into digital technology and practice. Other connections are dismantled and reassembled through novel conjunctions of technology, image and cultural expectations about digital visual communication. Some of these different photographies are directly related to each other, but others seem to weave together quite different objects, practices and processes. While all of this can be grouped together under the moniker 'digital photography', such a term belies the genuine complexity and diversity of how images, ideals and technologies are conceptualized, developed and used in different cultural contexts.

In chapters 1 and 2, I showed how the present ubiquity of photography, made possible through digitization, connects with a range of significant themes and issues in contemporary society and social thought. The proposed approach combined aspects of visual culture, consumption and technology worked through the notion of practice that tries to account for the specificity of digital photography on the ground and remains non-essentialist about what counts as photography. In a recent article Sarah Kember (2008) argues that photography is unlike other medium in that it is always in 'becoming' rather than *being*. There is some sense of this in attempting to show various kinds of stability and change in the proliferation and diversification of digital photography; there is little coherence in terms of a stable set of devices, ideals or practices here.

One of the purposes of organizing the book around chapters on image, technology and practice has been to separate these dimensions of ubiquitous photography in order to focus upon their specific dynamics. The second purpose has been to show how they are mutually entangled in reality. This may seem obvious, but, in reviewing much of the literature in chapter 2, we can see that there are forms of entrenchment within social theories of visual culture, consumption and technology that continue to privilege the production, content or use of images and the processes of commodification and consumption without reference to the dynamics of technology, or that conceptualize the technology as either a backdrop or a determining context for human action. In this way it has been important to consider these issues on their own terms, but also to articulate the ways in which they are mutually configured. The notion of *reconfiguration*, without reducing this to an institutional, technological or discursive process, has been the consistent motif throughout, illustrating the *ongoing potential* for moments of stability and change in photographic practices as they take the digital turn.

The efficacy of connecting images, technologies and ideals through a focus upon practice has been to show how change in one domain implies change in another. This does not mean that change necessarily occurs, however. As we have seen in chapters 3, 4 and 5, in some cases there are changes in technical design but not in the making or interpretation of the image. In others, technologies have replicated earlier ones, but have been used very differently in accordance with novel ideals. In chapter 3, I showed how several attributes of the digital image remain contested in practice, stemming from the multiplication of material forms the image can take and the ways in which they can be woven into different context of meaning and value. In chapter 4, we saw how processes of digitization and convergence are redistributing the agency of human and technical elements of the practice, generating new forms of skill and multiplying the potential trajectories of sociotechnical configuration. In chapter 5, the implications of the enfolding of photos in these networks were examined in relation to memory practices. I showed that multiple modes of memory-making are emerging which both reproduce and radically extend previous relations between photography, individual and collective memory.

Such a focus on the *local assembly* of these relations through how digital photography is practised might lead to a form of micro-empiricism that cannot tell us anything about digital culture more generally. This need not be the case at all, as the illustrations used throughout – drawn from detailed interview material, for example – have been used as precisely that: illustrations of the detail but also of the implications of that detail for more expansive theorizing about cultural change. Moreover, by focusing upon personal photography, it has hopefully been clear that, on the one hand, the cultural significance of this has been largely overlooked within intellectual circles and, on the other hand, has now become *viscerally* significant for the entire field of visual mediation in its cultural, sociopolitical and ethical dimensions. In line with this concern, in the remainder of this chapter I will simply suggest three ways in which details covered in the book raise such significant questions for the interpretation and critique of contemporary visual culture.

Photography and social change

I suggested in chapter 1 that personal photography provides an important arena for considering questions of stability and change. What are the relationships between photography and social change, and have these become more or less significant after digitization? There are several points of connection we can draw here. Firstly, photography – as an idea, a technology and a practice – has been subject *to* broader social change, whether that be shifts in socioeconomic, ethnic and gender relations over the nineteenth and twentieth centuries or the dynamics of population growth, movement and mobility, the rise of consumerism, the prevalence of military conflict, and so on. The nature of photography has altered in tandem with sweeping changes such as these. Secondly, theories and practices of photography were often central in *representing* such changes over the nineteenth and twentieth centuries, as they are now in the twenty-first century. Our understanding of the societal life of the last hundred and fifty years or so has been to a great extent *photographic*. Thirdly, photography and its continued ontological realism has been one of the most significant interventions in *promoting* social change precisely by making social realities visible and therefore available for reflection, inquiry and intervention. Finally, it can also be seen as key to our understanding *of* social change, both now and for future generations, partly because of its ubiquity but also because, by looking at how photography is practised (rather than only its products), we can observe significant social and technological change over the same period.

Bearing the above in mind, what is different about digital photography? I have documented some of the ways in which the ubiquity of cameras and other devices tells us a lot about the character of contemporary consumer culture, from the cultural norms of visual production and consumption to the ongoing specialization of visual technologies in relation to patterns of use and demand. The levels of documentation that arise through this have expanded exponentially through digitization, and, therefore, so has the potential for the visual understanding of the present. The sense in which ubiquitous photography can promote social change through the revealing of social and political realities – we return here again to Abu Ghraib – is as complex a question as it has ever been. While we can see that there is more visual mediation and greater visual knowledge of the world available, the question of how the politics of visual representation are actually managed remains a contested field of inquiry. While we can show how specific visual realities have been disseminated globally, we can also see that these are often absorbed and diffused by entrenched forms of political power. The field of vision, then, has become the central focus for the exercise of rhetorical and real power in the attempt to articulate normatively what society should look like. For example, at the present time there are a number of efforts to use digital images as the means to re-evaluate previous forms of photographic representation that are now seen as problematic. 'Project Naming', within Library and Archives Canada, displays and circulates digitized images of photographs of Inuit people taken in the early twentieth century in order to name the individuals present. In their original form, given the political context of the time, indigenous people were not individually 'named' but referred to as 'some natives'. The effort to rename these images, thereby altering the archival record, has been made possible through the networking of the images.

In terms of using practices of digital photography as a key to understanding broader dynamics of change, I have suggested that we can learn rather a lot about the technologization of ordinary social life, and that this in turn enables a reflection upon the modern categories of the domestic, of childhood, communication, memory, and so forth, and how they have always been tied to sociotechnical arrangements. We can see that practices of digital photography are inextricably enfolded into those of mobility. The new mobilities of contemporary societies are partly the outcome of, are shaped by, and contribute to the prevalence of mobile devices that have become new technologies of visual mediation (Elliott and Urry 2010). However, the more general diffusion of visual digital media in the bounded site of the domestic sphere (digital television, cameras, games, computing devices, and so on) appears to bring with it a series of significant impacts upon how family life is conducted and, perhaps even more pervasively, upon how we *think* of our social life.

Debates about these impacts often recycle previous ideas about how radio, television and computing would transform the organization of domestic spaces and practices, particularly the relations between parents and children (Postman 1982; Tapscott 1998). The general 'death of childhood' thesis (Buckingham 2000) sees new visual media as positioning children within adult worlds, which in turn invokes great parental anxiety as to the nature of childhood and the invention of new means of protection. We can observe this if we consider the increased use of cameras and cameraphones by children. For others, digital media open previously closed worlds, where the 'Net generation' is dramatically empowered to participate more fully in cultural life (Buckingham 2000). Moreover, it is thought that new media may strengthen rather than weaken existing family ties and democratic communication (Wellman and Haythornthwaite 2002). The sheer prevalence of digital visual technologies is implicated in all of these important debates, where, as I have shown, more people are involved in making basic decisions about visual mediation and representation and are subject to unprecedented levels of visual mediation in daily life. In this sense, digital photography can also operate as an exemplar of social change in terms of being situated at a dynamic intersection of technology and culture – a lens through which to articulate those relations.

Archiving, sending and sharing

The impact of digital photography in ordinary or daily life has been significant, as described throughout, and perhaps most clearly in relation to the notion that visual preservation has been all but replaced by *visual communication* (van Dijck 2007; Van House 2011). On the one hand, it has been assumed by film manufacturers such as Kodak that photography has always been about memory-making and sharing, and that there is no reason why this should not still be the case. On the other hand, there is an emerging consensus in scholarly debates, particularly within the information sciences and technology studies, that digital photography prioritizes communication over memorization (Van House et al. 2005; van Dijck 2007). The debates about analogue fixity and digital mobility are, I think, central to almost all terms of the debate about ubiquitous photography.

For instance, I have shown how specific ideals of permanence and fixity have been enfolded into the materials of photographic practice, from conceptions of light and nature, to the singularity of the print, to the processes of tagging and commenting that are often efforts to singularize, own or control the meaning of images in line with earlier photographic ideals. In terms of digitization, we have similarly seen ideals of circulation and ephemerality woven into the technologies, where the rationale of the image is sometimes one of distribution, and the causal snapping of thousands of images is valued as a means to develop new skills. I have suggested that, at times, these are abstractions that do not play out so uniformly at the level of practice. There is a relativity and cultural specificity to notions of permanence and ephemerality on the ground that needs to be taken more seriously and explored ethnographically in ways that I have suggested. Nonetheless, there is theoretical value in juxtaposing the idea of archiving and transmitting here, for it has particular relevance to the ways in which digital images are actually being managed for the future.

In ubiquitous photography, new forms of practice are emerging which combine forms of preservation and communication, sometimes as the result of intention (the simultaneous printing and uploading of the same photos, for example) and at other times the outcome of invisible processes of computation (how metadata structure the distribution of uploaded images). As discussed in chapter 3, it is often argued that issues of representation are mute in social media environments. The argument throughout has been that *both* trajectories are enabled and intensified through emerging sociotechnical practices of affective and self-conscious *distribution*. Most importantly, distribution involves not the reproduction of images but their *multiplication* and potential *variation*, their simultaneous dispersion and storage across a range of media, and, most significantly, their *ongoing* potential for remembering.

The convergence of multiple photographies with networked storage and distribution systems, alluded to in chapter 4 and explored in chapter 5, is producing a ubiquitous photoscape which brings together the habitual *and* event-orientated nature of memory-making. Of course, in juxtaposing the archive with the phenomenon of distribution or sharing, we are in danger of reifying a conceptualization of older memory practices as the rational organization of stable 'collections':

> As Halbwachs has so beautifully shown, we vest a good part of our archive in our lived environment . . . These traces do not fit nicely into our cultural understanding of the archive as a collection mediated by technology; however they are just as central to our recall of the past. In this modality, recall is not something committed to paper, print, or bytes, but is performed through lived experience. (Bowker et al. 2010: 213)

The point I am making here is that the ubiquitous photoscape of the Web, particularly the tagged visual landscape described in chapter 5, makes these historical relations explicit in ways that then allow for intensified reflexivity in our relations with the past and in the modes of engagement we have with our visual present. The most significant aspect of this, I think, is the collective production of potential memory by known and unknown others, as digital photos increase in number, circulate more widely, and are subject to interpretive intervention by combinations of people and software. But, as the collective aspect arises through configurations of humans and machines, does this negate collectivity and promote 'connectivity' (Hoskins 2009)? If we conceptualize memory practices as always already sociotechnical, then in asking what is different here I would argue that the dialectic of visible traces (the dynamic interface of, say, Facebook) and the invisible (metadata 'rules' structured by new media companies) produces multiple opportunities for the continual reworking of potential memories in ways that analogue technologies and techniques did not.

As discussed in the previous chapter, an emerging irony of so-called digital culture is the permanence of the past that is in a sense a new form of cultural *fixing*. Another aspect to this is the amount of detail being encoded into digital images at the level of the camera. The rise of location-aware technologies in general signifies a shift away from the notion of cyberspatial information towards dense informational forms of *local identification*. The increased use of smartphones at the present time represents an important reconfiguration of the image, with interconnected systems that fix images in terms of location, temporality and emerging forms of scheduling that constitute much 'mobile life'. The potentially dense visual material that arises as a result presents another trajectory in digital photography that reinforces its ubiquity.

The relationships between digital images, modes of circulation and mobility, and these new forms of software-generated fixity create a range of highly significant theoretical issues about memory and communication, but also seemingly intractable practical problems for those institutions attempting to order the visual landscape by developing robust classifications for cultural preservation.

Confessional culture, or, how to live publicly

The role of digital photography in the conduct of intimate social relationships has not been a primary focus of this book, but has been intimated through issues of ephemerality and durability, in the exponential increase in the number of images made and, perhaps most clearly, in the new visibilities of social relations in Flickr and Facebook. As regards these websites, the visual traces discussed above can also be considered in *ethical* terms. Those scholars working in cultural studies of media and communication, social network analysis, and the burgeoning field of social informatics have considered the ways in which individuals – particularly younger people – continually document and display aspects of their private lives to others (see Baym 2010). Within social theory, the seemingly *unavoidable* prevalence of uploading photos speaks most clearly to Bauman's (2007) notion of a 'confessional society', in which users constantly create and share content about the details of their private lives. In liquid modernity (Bauman 2000), a condition in which the mutuality of social bonds is continually reconfigured, there is a *will to confess* at work, a constant outpouring of detail about oneself that seems to represent the fluidity of identity formation and our continual (yet pointless) efforts to remake ourselves. This emphasis on self-presentation, particularly in popular writing about social media, often underpins a bemoaning of the 'lack of privacy' in contemporary visual culture. Similarly, in generally ahistorical popular journalism, there is a tendency simply to describe this seemingly incomprehensible landscape of minutiae and then position 'young people today' as increasingly narcissistic, obsessed with self-promotion and visually mediated appearances over the substance of 'real relationships'. While there are valid considerations to be made here – particularly the observation that younger generations engage in acts of visual communication on a scale that is unprecedented – I want to suggest that future research should consider how individuals

are developing a collectively orientated ethics for this landscape, rather than abandoning such a consideration in favour
of an individualized identity politics.

Acts of creation like this also produce traces of information such that the lives of others are knowable and visible to
an unprecedented degree. In other words, the creative visu-
alizations of ordinary things – intimate photos, conversations
and patterns of consumption – leave detailed impressions of
one's own and others' lives. Such impressions have become
commodities in their own right: fine-grained documents of
individuals to be bought and sold to marketing companies,
and also accounts of the daily lives of individuals 'of interest'
to bureaucratic and governmental institutions of one kind or
another. In this sense, the levels of transparency produced
have intensified the blurring or negation of public–private
boundaries constructed through modernity, whether that be
between the spheres of domestic life and work, the sacred and
the profane, government and the family, the visible and the
invisible, and so on.

In contrast to the notion that privacy should be recov-
ered or reinstated in some way, I want to suggest here that
a better question is *how can individuals live publicly?* Given
the accounts of photo-sharing in chapter 5, where individuals
talked about the perils and pitfalls of unmanageable images,
the apparent unavoidability for new generations of engaging
in visually mediated daily life introduces a series of potentially
novel ethical challenges and consequences with which young
people are currently engaging.

While issues of photographic image ownership and appropriation have of course been explored on ethical grounds, the
predominant focus of scholarship in this area revolves around
the effects of *misrepresentation* or affected experiences of
trauma (Butler 2007; Hirsch and Valentino 2001) in ways that
the aforementioned Project Naming seeks to re-evaluate. The
convergence of photography and online social media environments has in some ways reinforced these ethical foundations

but has also made an additional range of ethical thought *visible*. Online photo-sharing practices not only demand a reactive, after-the-fact ethics, but also present a space for the consideration of new modes of 'affective responsibility' (Hand and Scarlett 2009). In the event of photo-sharing, software manipulates the means and contexts through which images are presented, engaged with and represented. As we have seen, these characteristics are often dealt with through the practices of selective uploading, tagging, de-tagging, commenting and deletion that are integral components of social networking software. As discussed, these practices enable users *continually* to monitor their public image while simultaneously acting as prosumers who are responsible for configuring and reconfiguring the networked connections drawn between particular images, individuals and things. What is at stake is not only the negotiation of the representational elements of the image but also *what the image is communicating.*

Given the potential implications of visual communication on this scale and at this fine-grained level of personal detail, the identities of suspecting and unsuspecting, expected and unexpected visitors, the performative act of photo-sharing carries significant ethical consequence. What is suggestive from the exploratory work done here is how individuals are moving away from a traditional view of ethics, as a series of core (and often moralistic) principles that facilitate risk minimization, towards an approach with poststructuralist inclinations which positions ethics as a matter of irreducible responsibility and unrequited hospitality towards the (unexpected) Other. This is often acknowledged to some degree through individuals' discussions regarding the public and somewhat uncontrollable nature of social networking sites, surveillance and authorship. Students spoke of being mindful of the potential for unintended and negative consequences when selecting and engaging with images of others; several individuals spoke about minimizing their interaction with images of others (by either not posting or not tagging) in an effort to reduce the possibility of harming them. While it in many ways points to an ethics of hospitality (Derrida 1994; Secomb 2006), individuals uphold this when handling images of other people but return to an ethics of individual responsibility when monitoring the management of their own images by others. The immanent construction of an ethics of ubiquitous photography encompasses and combines several traditions – the ethical critique of representation linked to institutional power, the liberal rights and responsibilities model of individual action, and also the new affective responsibilities developed in relation to the tagged visual landscape.

As photography is woven into emerging sociotechnical systems, new ethical challenges and dilemmas arise. The future of digital photography is of course uncertain, embodying many possible trajectories as standardization of digital imaging continues across devices, systems and forms of ordinary practice. It seems highly unlikely that we will see a decrease in the significance of visual mediation in the near future, and, as such, scholars will need to develop new approaches to new phenomena, paying as much attention to the lived experiences of those producing and engaging with these phenomena as to established accounts of digital media and society.

References and Bibliography

Adorno, T., and Horkheimer, M. (1972) *The Dialectic of Enlightenment*, trans. J. Cumming. New York: Herder & Herder.

Akrich, M. (1992) 'The de-scription of technical objects', in *Shaping Technology/Building Society: Studies in Sociotechnical Change*, ed. W. Bijker and J. Law. Cambridge, MA: MIT Press, pp. 205–25.

Arvidsson, A. (2005) *Brands: Meaning and Value in Media Culture*. New York: Routledge.

Barney, D. (2004) *The Network Society*. Cambridge: Polity.

Barry, A. (2001) *Political Machines: Governing a Technological Society*. New York: Athlone Press.

Barthes, R. (1973) *The Pleasure of the Text*. New York: Macmillan.

Barthes, R. (1977) *Music, Image, Text: Selected Essays*. New York: Hill & Wang.

Barthes, R. (1982) *Camera Lucida: Reflections on Photography*. New York: Hill & Wang.

Batchen, G. (2002) *Each Wild Idea: Writing, Photography, History*. Cambridge, MA: MIT Press.

Bate, D. (2009) *Photography: The Key Concepts*. Oxford. Berg.

Baudelaire, C. ([1859] 1980) 'On photography', in *Classic Essays on Photography*, ed. A. Trachtenberg. New Haven, CT: Leete's Island Books.

Baudrillard, J. (1970) *The Consumer Society: Myths and Structures*. London: Sage.

Baudrillard, J. (1981) *For a Critique of the Political Economy of the Sign*. London: Sage.

Baudrillard, J. (1988) *Selected Writings*, ed. M. Poster. Cambridge: Polity.

Bauman, Z. (1990) *Globalization: The Human Consequences*. Cambridge: Polity.

Bauman, Z. (2000) *Liquid Modernity*. Cambridge: Polity.

Bauman, Z. (2001) *The Individualized Society*. Cambridge: Polity.

Bauman, Z. (2007) *Consuming Life*. Cambridge: Polity.

Baylis, G. (2008) 'Remediations: or when is a boring photograph not a boring photograph', *Photographies*, 1(1): 29–48.

Baym, N. (2010) *Personal Connections in the Digital Age*. Cambridge: Polity.

Bazin, A. (1967) 'The ontology of the photograph', in *What is Cinema?* Berkeley: University of California Press.

Beer, D. (2009) 'Power through the algorithm? Participatory web cultures and the technological unconscious', *New Media and Society*, 11(6): 985–1002.

Beer, D. (2010) 'Mobile music, coded objects, and everyday spaces', *Mobilities*, 5(4): 469–84.

Beer, D., and Burrows, R. (2007) 'Sociology of, and in Web 2.0', *Sociological Research Online*, 12(5).

Beer, D., and Burrows, R. (2010) 'Consumption, presumption and participatory web cultures', *Journal of Consumer Culture*, 10(1): 3–12.

Benjamin, W. ([1931] 1979) 'A small history of photography', in *One Way Street and Other Writings*, trans. E. Jephcott and K. Shorter. London: New Left Books, pp. 240–57.

Benjamin, W. (1999a) 'The work of art in the age of mechanical reproduction', in *Illuminations*, ed. H. Arendt. London: Pimlico.

Benjamin, W. (1999b) "On some motifs in Baudelaire', in *Illuminations*, ed. H. Arendt. London: Pimlico.

Benjamin, W. (1999c) 'Unpacking my library', in *Illuminations*, ed. H. Arendt. London: Pimlico.

Benner, M., and Tripsas, M. (2010) *The Influence of Prior Industry Affiliation on Framing in Nascent Industries: The Evolution of Digital Cameras*, Harvard Business School Working Paper no. 11-007, available at: http://www.hbs.edu/research/pdf/11-007.pdf.

Berger, J. (1972) *Ways of Seeing*. London: Penguin.

Berger, J., and Mohr, J. (1982) *Another Way of Telling*. New York: Pantheon.

Bijker, W. (1992) 'The social construction of fluorescent lighting, or how an artifact was invented in its diffusion stage', in *Shaping Technology/Building Society: Studies in Sociotechnical Change*, ed. W. Bijker and J. Law. Cambridge, MA: MIT Press, pp. 75–104.

Bijker, W. (1995) *Of Bicycles, Bakelites and Bulbs: Toward a Theory of Sociotechnical Change*. Cambridge, MA: MIT Press.

Bijker, W., and Law, J., eds (1992) *Shaping Technology/Building Society: Studies in Sociotechnical Change*. Cambridge, MA: MIT Press.

Bijker, W., Hughes, T. P., and Pinch, T. (1987) *The Social Construction of Technological Systems: New Directions in the Sociology and History of Technology*. Cambridge, MA: MIT Press.

Bolter, J. D., and Grusin, R. (1999) *Remediation: Understanding New Media*. Cambridge, MA: MIT Press.

Bourdieu, P. (1984) *Distinction: A Social Critique of the Judgement of Taste*. Cambridge, MA: Harvard University Press.

Bourdieu, P. (1990a) *Photography: A Middle Brow Art*. Cambridge: Polity.

Bourdieu, P. (1990b) *The Logic of Practice*. Cambridge: Polity.

Bowker, G. (2005) *Memory Practices in the Sciences*. Cambridge, MA: MIT Press.

Bowker, G., and Star, S. (1999) *Sorting Things Out: Classification and its Consequences*. Cambridge, MA: MIT Press.

Bowker, G., Baker, K., Millerand, F., and Ribes, D. (2010) 'Toward information infrastructure studies: ways of knowing in a networked environment', in J. Hunsinger, L. Klastrup and M. Allen, eds, *International Handbook of Internet Research*. Dordrecht and London: Springer, pp. 97–117.

Brockmeier, J. (2010) 'After the archive: remapping memory', *Culture and Psychology*, 16(1): 5–35.

Buckingham, D. (2000) *After the Death of Childhood: Growing up in the Age of Electronic Media*. Cambridge: Polity.

Buckley, C. (1986) 'Made in patriarchy: toward a feminist analysis of women and design', *Design Issues*, 3(2): 3–14.

Burgess, J., and Green, J. (2009) *YouTube: Online Video and Participatory Culture*. Cambridge: Polity.

Burgin, V. (1996) *In/Different Spaces: Place and Memory in Visual Culture*. Berkeley: University of California Press.

Buse, P. (2010) 'Polaroid into digital: technology, cultural form, and the social practices of snapshot photography', *Continuum*, 24: 215–30.

Butler, J. (2007) 'Torture and the ethics of photography', *Environment and Planning D: Society and Space*, 25: 951–66.

Bywater, Michael (2010) 'The age of mass narcissism', *The Independent*, 12 May.

Cadava, E. (1999) *Words of Light*. Princeton, NJ: Princeton University Press.

Campbell, C. (2005) 'The craft consumer: culture, craft and consumption in a postmodern society', *Journal of Consumer Culture*, 5(1): 23–41.

Castells, M. (1996) *The Information Age: Economy, Society and Culture*, Vol. 1: *The Rise of the Network Society*. Oxford: Blackwell.

Castells, M. (2010) *The Information Age: Economy, Society, and Culture*, Vol. 3: *End of Millennium*. 2nd edn, Oxford: Blackwell.

Certeau, M. de (1984) *The Practice of Everyday Life*. Berkeley: University of California Press.

Chalfen, R. (1987) *Snapshot Versions of Life*. Bowling Green, OH: Bowling Green State University Popular Press.

Chaney, D. (1996) *Lifestyles*. London: Routledge.

Clarke, G. (1997) *The Photograph*. Oxford: Oxford University Press.

Cobley, N., and Haeffner, P. (2009) 'Digital cameras and domestic photography: communication, agency, and structure', *Visual Communication*, 8(2): 123–46.

Cohen, A. (2007) 'Photography's histories', in J. Elkins, ed., *Photography Theory*. London: Routledge.

Cohen, K. (2003) 'What does the photoblog want?', *Media, Culture, and Society*, 27(6): 883–901.

Collins, J. (1995) *Architectures of Excess: Cultural Life in the Information Age*. London: Routledge.

Crary, J. (1990) *Techniques of the Observer: On Vision and Modernity in the Nineteenth Century*. Cambridge: MA: MIT Press.

Crary, J. (1991) 'Capital effects', *High/Low: Art and Mass Culture*, 56: 121–51.

Crary, J. (1993) *Incorporations: Zone 6*. Cambridge, MA: MIT Press.

Cronin, A. (2004) *Advertising Myths: The Strange Half-Lives of Images and Commodities*. London: Routledge.

Csikszentmihalyi, M., and Rochberg-Halton, E. (1981) *The Meaning of Things: Domestic Symbols and the Self*. Cambridge: Cambridge University Press.

Daisuke, O., and Ito, M. (2003) 'Technosocial situations: emergent structuring of mobile email use', *Journal of Socio-Information Studies*, 7: 97–111.

Dant, T. (1999) *Material Culture in the Social World: Values, Activities, Lifestyles*. Buckingham: Open University Press.

Dant, T. (2005) *Materiality and Society*. Maidenhead: Open University Press.

Debord, G. (1983) *Society of the Spectacle*. London: Rebel Press.

de Rijcke, S. (2010) 'Regarding the brain: practices of objectivity in cerebral imaging, 17th century – present', PhD thesis, University of Groningen.

Derrida, J. (1994) *The Politics of Friendship*, trans. George Collins. New York: Verso.

Dodge, M., and Kitchen, R. (2008) *Software, Objects and Home Space*, National Institute for Regional and Spatial Analysis, Working Paper no. 35; available at: http://eprints.nuim.ie/1150/1/NIRSAWP35Software_objects_and_home_spaceDodge.pdf.

Dunleavy, D. (2005) 'Photojournalism and the digital camera: thirty years and counting', available at: http://ddunleavy.typepad.com/ the_big_picture/2005/10/the_digital_cam.html.

Dunn, R. G. (2008) *Identifying Consumption*. Philadelphia: Temple University Press.

Edwards, E., and Hart, J. eds (2004) *Photographs, Objects, Histories: On the Materiality of Images*. London: Routledge.

Edwards, S. (2006) *Photography: A Very Short Introduction*. Oxford: Oxford University Press.

Elkins, J., ed. (2007) *Photography Theory*. London: Routledge.

Elliott, A., and Urry, J. (2010) *Mobile Lives*. London: Routledge.

Ewen, S. (1976) *Captains of Consciousness: Advertising and the Social Roots of the Consumer Culture*. New York: McGraw-Hill.

Featherstone, M. (2000) 'Archiving cultures', *British Journal of Sociology*, 51(1): 161–84.

Featherstone, M. (2007) *Consumer Culture and Postmodernism*. London: Sage.

Finn, J. M. (2009) *Capturing the Criminal Image: From Mug Shot to Surveillance Society*. Minneapolis: University of Minnesota Press.

Foster, H. (1988) *Vision and Visuality*. Seattle: Bay Press.

Foucault, M. (1977) *Discipline and Punish*. London: Tavistock Press.

Foucault, M. (1984) *The Foucault Reader*, ed. P. Rabinow. London: Pantheon Books.

Fox-Talbot, H. ([1844] 1981) *The Pencil of Nature*. London: Longman.

Frosh, P. (2003) *The Image Factory*. Oxford: Berg.

Gane, N. (2006) 'Speed-up or slow down? Social theory in the information age', *Information, Communication and Society*, 9(1): 20–38.

Gane, N., and Beer, D. (2008) *New Media: The Key Concepts*. Oxford: Berg.

Gane, N., Venn, C., and Hand, M. (2007) 'Ubiquitous surveillance', *Theory, Culture & Society*, 24(7–8): 349–58.

Gere, C. (2002) *Digital Culture*. London: Reaktion Books.

Giddens, A. (1984) *The Constitution of Society*. Berkeley: University of California Press.

Giddens, A. (1991) *Modernity and Self-Identity: Self and Society in the Late Modern Age*. Cambridge: Polity.

Giddens, A. (1994) *Beyond Left and Right: The Future of Radical Politics*. Cambridge: Polity.

Gillis, J. R. (1994) 'Memory and identity: the history of a relationship', in J. R. Gillis, ed., *Commemorations: The Politics of National Identity*. Princeton,NJ: Princeton University Press, pp. 3–24.

Goggin, G. (2006) *Cell Phone Culture: Mobile Technology in Everyday Life*. London: Routledge.

Grint, K., and Woolgar, S. (1997) *The Machine at Work: Technology, Work, and Organization.* Cambridge: Polity.

Grunow, J., and Warde, A., eds (2001) *Ordinary Consumption.* London: Routledge.

Gunthert, A. (2008) 'Digital imaging goes to war: the Abu Ghraib photographs', *Photographies*, 1(1): 103–12.

Halbwachs, M. (1992) *On Collective Memory.* Chicago: University of Chicago Press.

Hall, S., ed. (1997) *Representation: Cultural Representations and Signifying Practices.* London: Sage and Open University Press.

Hand, M. (2008) *Making Digital Cultures: Access, Interactivity, and Authenticity.* Aldershot: Ashgate.

Hand, M. (2010) 'The rise and fall of cyberspace, or how cyberspace turned inside out', in J. Hall, L. Grindstaff and L. Ming-Cheng, eds, *Handbook of Cultural Sociology.* London: Routledge.

Hand, M., and Scarlett, A. (2009) 'Photo-sharing and performativity', paper presented at the annual meeting of the Society for Social Studies of Science, Washington, DC, October.

Hand, M., and Shove, E. (2004) 'Orchestrating concepts: kitchen dynamics and regime change in *Good Housekeeping* and *Ideal Home*, 1922–2002', *Home Cultures*, 1(3): pp. 1–22.

Hand, M., and Shove, E. (2007) 'Condensing practices: ways of living with the freezer', *Journal of Consumer Culture*, 7(1): 79–104.

Hardey, M. (2007) 'The city in the age of Web 2.0: a new synergistic relationship between place and people', *Information, Communication & Society*, 10(6): 867–84.

Harvey, D. (1989) *The Urban Experience.* Baltimore: Johns Hopkins University Press.

Harvey, D. (1990) *The Condition of Postmodernity: An Enquiry into the Origins of Cultural Change.* Oxford: Blackwell.

Hassan, R. (2008) *The Information Society.* Cambridge: Polity.

Hayles, N. K. (1999) *How We Became Post-Human: Virtual Bodies in Cybernetics, Literature, and Informatics.* Chicago: University of Chicago Press.

Hayles, N. K. (2005) *My Mother Was a Computer: Digital Subjects and Literary Texts.* Chicago: University of Chicago Press.

Henning, M. (2007) 'New lamps for old: photography, obsolescence and social change', in C. Acland, ed., *Residual Media.* Minneapolis: University of Minnesota Press.

Heywood, I., and Sandywell, B., eds (2011) *The Handbook of Visual Culture.* Oxford: Berg.

Hirsch, F. (1976) *Social Limits to Growth*. Cambridge, MA: Harvard University Press.

Hirsch, J. (1981) *Family Photography: Context, Meaning and Effect*. Oxford: Oxford University Press.

Hirsch, M. (1997) *Family Frames: Photography, Narrative, and Postmemory*. Cambridge, MA: Harvard University Press.

Hirsch, R. (2000) *Seizing the Light: A History of Photography*. Toronto: McGraw-Hill.

Hirsch, R., and Valentino, J. (2001) *Photographic Possibilities: The Expressive Use of Ideas, Material, and Processes*. London: Focal Press.

Holland, P. (2009) 'Sweet it is to scan: personal photographs and popular photography', in L. Wells, ed., *Photography: A Critical Introduction*. London: Routledge.

Holt, D. (2004) *How Brands Become Icons: The Principles of Cultural Branding*. Boston: Harvard Business School.

Horst, H., and Miller, D. (2006) *The Cell Phone: An Anthropology of Communication*. Oxford: Berg.

Hoskins, A. (2007) *Media and Memory*. London: Routledge.

Hoskins, A. (2009) 'Digital network memory', in A. Erll and A. Rigney, eds, *Mediation, Remediation, and the Dynamics of Cultural Memory*. Berlin: Walter de Gruyter.

Idhe, D. (1995) *Postphenomenology: Essays in the Postmodern Context*. Evanston, IL: Northwestern University Press.

Jack, I. (2009) 'The unstoppable rise of the citizen cameraman', *The Guardian*, 11 April.

Jameson, F. (1990) *Signatures of the Visible*. New York: Routledge.

Jameson, F. (1991) *Postmodernism, or, The Cultural Logic of Late Capitalism*. Durham, NC: Duke University Press.

Jansson, A. (2002) 'The mediatization of consumption', *Journal of Consumer Culture*, 2(1): 5–31.

Jay, M. (1993) *Force Fields: Between Intellectual History and Cultural Change*. London: Routledge.

Jedlowski, P. (2001) 'Memory and sociology', *Time and Society*, 10(1): 29–44.

Jeffries, S. (2010) 'The rise of the camera-phone', *The Guardian*, 8 January.

Jenkins, H. (2006) *Convergence Culture: Where Old and New Media Collide*. New York: New York University Press.

Jenks, C. (1995) *Visual Culture*. London: Routledge.

Julier, G. (2000) *The Culture of Design*. London: Sage.

Keegan, V. (2006) 'Snapshot of the true content generators', *The Guardian*, 30 November.

Keegan, V. (2008) 'Snap! Cameraphones keep getting better', *The Guardian*, 6 November.

Keen, A. (2007) *The Cult of the Amateur: How Today's Internet is Killing our Culture*. London: Doubleday.

Kember, S. (1995) 'Medicine's new vision', in M. Lister, ed., *The Photographic Image in Digital Culture*. London: Routledge, pp. 115–28.

Kember, S. (1998) *Virtual Anxiety: Photography, New Technologies, and Subjectivity*. Manchester: Manchester University Press.

Kember, S. (2003) *Cyberfeminism and Artificial Life*. London: Routledge.

Kember, S. (2008) 'The virtual life of photography', *Photographies*, 1(2): 175–203.

King, G. (1986) *Say 'Cheese'! Looking at Snapshots in a New Way*. New York: Dodds Mead.

Klein, N. (2000) *No Logo: Taking Aim at the Brand Bullies*. New York: Picador.

Kopytoff, I. (1986) 'The cultural biography of things: commoditization as process', in A. Appadurai, ed., *The Social Life of Things*. Cambridge: Cambridge University Press.

Kracauer, S. (1965) *Theory of Film: The Redemption of Physical Reality*. Princeton, NJ: Princeton University Press.

Lally, E. (2002) *At Home with Computers*. Oxford: Berg.

Lasch, C. (1979) *The Culture of Narcissism*. New York: W. W. Norton.

Lash, S. (2002) *Critique of Information*. London: Sage.

Lash, S. (2007) 'Power after hegemony: cultural studies in mutation', *Theory, Culture & Society*, 24(3): 55–78.

Lash, S., and Lury, C. (2007) *Global Culture Industry: The Mediation of Things*. Cambridge: Polity.

Lash, S., and Urry, J. (1994) *Economies of Signs and Space*. London: Sage.

Latour, B. (1991) 'Technology is society made durable', in J. Law, ed., *A Sociology of Monsters: Essays on Power, Technology and Domination*. London: Routledge, pp. 103–31.

Latour, B. (1992) 'Where are the missing masses? A sociology of a few mundane artifacts', in W. Bijker and J. Law, eds, *Shaping Technology/ Building Society*. Cambridge, MA: MIT Press, pp. 225–58.

Latour, B. (1993) *We Have Never Been Modern*. Hemel Hempstead: Harvester Wheatsheaf.

Latour, B. (1996) 'On interobjectivity', *Mind, Culture, and Activity*, 3: 28–45.

Latour, B. (1999) *Pandora's Hope: Essays on the Reality of Science Studies*. Cambridge, MA: Harvard University Press.

Latour, B. (2000) 'When things strike back: a possible contribution of "science studies" to the social sciences', *British Journal of Sociology*, 51(1): 107–23.

Latour, B. (2005) *Reassembling the Social: An Introduction to Actor-Network Theory*. Oxford: Oxford University Press.

Latour, B. (2007) 'Beware, your imagination leaves digital traces', *Times Higher Education Supplement*, 6 April.

Law, J. (1991) 'Monsters, machines and sociotechnical relations', in J. Law, ed., *A Sociology of Monsters*. London: Routledge.

Law, J. (1994) *Organizing Modernity*. Oxford: Blackwell.

Law, J. (2004) *After Method: Mess in Social Science Research*. Abingdon: Routledge.

Law, J. (2008) 'On sociology and STS', *Sociological Review*, 56: 623–49.

Law, J., and Hassard, J., eds (1999) *Actor Network Theory and After*. Oxford: Blackwell.

Leach, W. (1993) *Land of Desire: Merchants, Power, and the Rise of a New American Culture*. New York: Pantheon Books.

Leadbeater, C. (2008) *We-think*. London: Profile.

Lears, J. (1994) *Fables of Abundance: A Cultural History of Advertising in America*. New York: Basic Books.

Lee, D.-H. (2009) 'Mobile snapshots and public/private boundaries', *Knowledge, Technology & Policy*, 22(3): 161–71.

Leiss, W., Kline, S., Jhally, S., and Botterill, J. (2005) *Social Communication in Advertising: Consumption in the Mediated Marketplace*. 3rd edn, New York and London: Routledge.

Lenhardt, A., and Madden, M. (2005) 'Teen content creators and consumers', Pew Internet and American Life Project, available at: http://pewinternet.org/Reports/2005/Teen-Content-Creators-and-Consumers.aspx.

Lerman, K., and Jones, L. (2006) 'Social browsing on Flickr', *Proceedings of the International Conference on Weblogs and Social Media*, available at: http://arxiv.org/PS_cache/cs/pdf/0612/0612047v1.pdf.

Ling, R., and Donner, J. (2009) *Mobile Communication*. Cambridge: Polity.

Lister, M., ed. (1995) *The Photographic Image in Digital Culture*. London: Routledge.

Lister, M. (2000) 'Photography in the age of electronic media', in *Photography: A Critical Introduction*, ed. L. Wells. 2nd edn, London: Routledge, pp. 305–45.

Lister, M. (2007) 'Sack in the sand', *Convergence*, 13(3): 251–74.

Lister, M., Dovey, J., Grant, I., and Kelly, K. (2003) *New Media: A Critical Introduction*. London: Routledge.

Lister, M., Dovey, J., Giddings, S., and Grant, I. (2009) *New Media: A Critical Introduction*. 2nd edn, London: Routledge.

Loeb, L. A. (1994) *Consuming Angels: Advertising and Victorian Women*. Oxford: Oxford University Press.

Lundby, K., ed. (2009) *Mediatization: Concept, Changes, Consequences*. Oxford: Peter Lang.

Lunenfeld, P. (2000a) *The Digital Dialectic: New Essays on New Media*. Cambridge, MA: MIT Press.

Lunenfeld, P. (2000b) *Snap to Grid*. Cambridge, MA: MIT Press.

Lury, C. (1992) *Cultural Rights: Technology, Legality and Personality*. London: Routledge.

Lury, C. (1996) *Consumer Culture*. Cambridge: Polity.

Lury, C. (1998) *Prosthetic Culture: Photography, Memory, and Identity*. London: Routledge.

Lury, C. (2004) *Brands: The Logos of the Global Economy*. London and New York: Routledge.

Lyman, P., and Varian, H. R. (2003) *How Much Information?*, available at: http://www2.sims.berkeley.edu/research/projects/how-much-info-2003/.

Lyon, D. (2001) *Surveillance Society: Monitoring Everyday Life*. Buckingham: Open University Press.

Lyon, D. (2007) *Surveillance Studies: An Overview*. Cambridge: Polity.

Lyotard, J.-F. (1984) *The Postmodern Condition: A Report on Knowledge*. Minneapolis: University of Minnesota Press.

McFall, L. (2004) *Advertising: A Cultural Economy*. London: Sage.

McGuigan, J. (1988) *Cultural Populism*. London: Routledge.

Manovich, L. (2001) *The Language of New Media*. Cambridge, MA: MIT Press.

Manovich, L. ([1995] 2003) "The paradoxes of digital photography," in *The Photography Reader*, ed. L. Wells. London and New York: Routledge.

Manovich, L. (2008) *Software Takes Command*, book draft, available at: http://lab.softwarestudies.com/2008/11/softbook.html.

Marien, M. W. (1997) *Photography and its Critics: A Cultural History, 1839–1900*. Cambridge: Cambridge University Press.

Marien, M. W. (2006) *Photography: A Cultural History*. 2nd edn, London: Laurence King.

Marwick, A. E., and boyd, d. (2011) 'The drama! Teen conflict, gossip, and bullying in networked publics', paper given at *A Decade in Internet Time: Symposium on the Dynamics of the Internet and Society*, September; available at Social Science Research Network: http://ssrn.com/abstract=1926349.

Meyer, E. (2008) 'Digital photography', in K. St Amant and S. Kelsey, eds, *Handbook of Research on Computer Mediated Communication*. New York: Hershey.

Miller, D. (1997) 'Consumption and its consequences', in H. Mackay, ed., *Consumption and Everyday Life*. London: Sage and Open University Press.

Miller, D. (2011) *Tales from Facebook*. Cambridge: Polity.

Miller, D., and Slater, D. (2000) *The Internet: An Ethnographic Approach*. Oxford: Berg.

Misa, T. J. (2004) *Leonardo to the Internet: Technology and Culture from the Renaissance to the Present*. Baltimore: Johns Hopkins University Press.

Mitchell, W. J. (1992) *The Reconfigured Eye: Visual Truth in the Post-Photographic Era*. Cambridge, MA: MIT Press.

Moor, L. (2007) *The Rise of Brands*. Oxford and New York: Berg.

Mosco, V. (2009) *The Political Economy of Communication*. 2nd edn, London: Sage.

Murray, S. (2008) 'Digital images, photo-sharing, and our shifting notions of everyday aesthetics'. *Journal of Visual Culture*, 7(2): 147–63.

Nizza, M., and Lyons, P. J. (2008) 'In an Iranian image, a missile too many', *New York Times* blog, available at: http://thelede.blogs.nytimes.com/2008/07/10/in-an-iranian-image-a-missile-too-many/?hp.

Olick, J. K. (2007) *The Politics of Regret: On Collective Memory and Historical Responsibility*. London: Routledge.

O'Reilly, T. (2005) 'What is Web 2.0: design patterns and business models for the next generation of software', available at: http://oreilly.com/web2/archive/what-is-web-20.html.

Osborne, P. (2010) 'Infinite exchange: the social ontology of the photographic image', *Philosophy of Photography*, 1(1): 59–68.

Osborne, T. (1999) 'The ordinariness of the archive', *History of the Human Sciences*, 12(2): 51–64

Oudshoorn, N., and Pinch, T. (2002) *How Users Matter: the Co-Construction of Users and Technology*. Cambridge, MA: MIT Press.

Parke, R. L. (2003) 'Basic evidence photography (and my case for "going digital")', http://www.nalionline.org/docs/Parke_Evidence_Photography.pdf.

Pauwels, L. (2008) 'A private visual practice going public? Social functions and sociological research opportunities of web-based family photography', *Visual Studies*, 23: 34–49.

Peirce, C. (1955) *Philosophical Writings of Peirce*. New York: Dover.

Poster, M. (1990) *The Mode of Information: Poststructuralism and Social Context*. Cambridge: Polity.

Poster, M. (1995) *The Second Media Age*. Cambridge: Polity.

Poster, M. (2006) *Information Please*. Durham, NC: Duke University Press.

Postman, N. (1982) *The Disappearance of Childhood*. New York: Delacorte Press.

Putnam, R. (2001) *Bowling Alone*. New York: Simon & Schuster.

Ritchin, F. (1990) *In our own Image: The Coming Revolution in Photography*. New York: Aperture.

Ritzer, G. (2010) *The McDonaldization of Society*. London: Sage.

Robins, K. (1991) 'Into the image: visual technologies and vision cultures, in P. Wombell, ed., *Photovideo: Photography in the Age of the Computer*. London: Rivers Oram Press.

Robins, K. (1995) 'Will images move us still?', in *The Photographic Image in Digital Culture*. New York: Routledge, pp. 29–49.

Rose, G. (2004) '"Everyone's cuddled up and it just looks really nice": an emotional geography of some mums and their family photos', *Social & Cultural Geography*, 5(4): 549–64.

Rosen, P. (2001) *Change Mummified: Cinema, Historicity, Theory*. Minneapolis: University of Minnesota Press.

Rosler, M. (1991) 'In, around and afterthoughts (on documentary photography)', in R. Bolton, ed., *The Contest of Meaning: Critical Histories of Photography*. Cambridge, MA: MIT Press.

Rubenstein, D., and Sluis, K. (2008) 'A life more photographic', *Photographies*, 1(1): 9–28.

Ruby, J. (2005) 'The last 20 years of visual anthropology – a critical review', *Visual Studies*, 20(2): 159–70.

Sandywell, B. (2004) 'The myth of everyday life: toward a heterology of the ordinary', *Cultural Studies*, 18(2–3): 160–80.

Sandywell, B. (2011) *Dictionary of Visual Discourse: A Dialectical Lexicon of Terms*. Oxford: Berg.

Sassatelli, R. (2007) *Consumer Culture: History, Theory, Politics*. London: Sage.

Sassoon, D. (2004) *Becoming Mona Lisa: The Making of a Global Icon*. Darby, PA: Diane.

Savage, M., and Burrows, R. (2007) 'The coming crisis of empirical sociology', *Sociology*, 41(5): 885–99.

Scarlett, A. (2010) 'Remediating photography: re-imagining ethics in light of online photo-sharing practices', MA thesis, Queen's University; available at: http://qspace.library.queensu.ca/handle/1974/6113.

Schroeder, J. E. (2002) *Visual Consumption*. London: Routledge.

Schwartz, J. (1995) '"We make our tools and our tools make us": lessons from photographs for the practice, politics, and poetics of diplomatics', *Archiveria*, 40 (fall): 40–74.

Schwartz, J., and Cook, T. (2002) 'Archives, records, and power: from (postmodern) theory to (archival) performance', *Archival Science*, 2: 171–85.

Secomb, L. (2006) 'Amorous politics: between Derrida and Nancy', *Social Semiotics*, 16(3): 449–60.

Sekula, A. (1989) 'The body and the archive', in R. Bolton, ed., *The Contest of Meaning: Critical Histories of Photography*. Cambridge, MA: MIT Press.

Shapin, S. (1990) *A Social History of Truth*. Chicago: University of Chicago Press.

Shove, E. (2003) *Comfort, Cleanliness and Convenience: The Social Organization of Normality*. Oxford: Berg.

Shove, E., Watson, M., Hand, M., and Ingram, J. (2007) *The Design of Everyday Life*. Oxford: Berg

Silverstone, R. (1993) 'Time, information and communication technologies in the household', *Time and Society*, 2(3): 283–311.

Silverstone, R. (2007)   *Media and Morality: On the Rise of the Mediapolis*. Cambridge: Polity.

Silverstone, R., Hirsch, E., and Morley, D. (1992) 'Information and communication technologies and the moral economy of the household', in R. Silverstone and E. Hirsch, eds, *Consuming Technologies*. London: Routledge.

Sismondo, S. (2009) *An Introduction to Science and Technology Studies*. Oxford: Blackwell.

Slater, D. (1985) 'Marketing mass photography', in H. Davis and P. Walton, eds, *Language, Image, Media*. Oxford: Blackwell, pp. 245–63.

Slater, D. (1991) 'Consuming Kodak', in J. Spence and P. Holland, eds, *Family Snaps: The Meanings of Domestic Photography*. London: Virago.

Slater, D. (1995) 'Domestic photography and digital culture', in M. Lister, ed., *The Photographic Image in Digital Culture*. London: Routledge.

Slater, D. (1997) *Consumer Culture and Modernity*. Cambridge: Polity.

Smart, B. (2010) *Consumer Society: Critical Issues and Environmental Consequences*. London: Sage.

Solomun, S. (2011) 'A mobile army of metaphors: from archiving to sharing in digital photographic practice', *Proceedings of the 9th International Conference on New Directions in the Humanities*, 8–11 June.

Sontag, S. (1977) *On Photography*. Harmondsworth: Penguin.

Sontag, S. (1979) *Illness as Metaphor*. New York: Vintage Books.

Sontag, S. (2004) 'Regarding the torture of others', *New York Times*, 23 May.

Sparke, P. (1986) *Furniture: Twentieth-Century Design*. London: Bell & Hyman.

Spence, J., and Holland, P. (1991) *Family Snaps: The Meaning of Domestic Photography*. London: Virago.

Sturken, M., and Cartwright, L. (2008) *Practices of Looking: An Introduction to Visual Culture*. Oxford: Oxford University Press.

Tagg, J. (1988) *The Burden of Representation: Essays on Photographies and Histories*. Amherst: University of Massachusetts Press.

Tagg, J. (1993) *Grounds of Dispute: Art History, Cultural Politics and the Discursive Field*. London: Macmillan.

Tapscott, D. (1998) *Growing Up Digital: The Rise of the Net Generation*. New York: McGraw-Hill.

Taylor, P., and Harris, J. (2005) *Digital Matters: The Theory and Culture of the Matrix*. London and New York: Routledge.

Thompson, J. (2005) 'The new visibility', *Theory, Culture & Society*, 22(6): 31–51.

Thrift, N. (2005) *Knowing Capitalism*. London: Sage.

Thrift, N. (2008) *Non-Representational Theory*. London: Routledge.

Trottier, D. (2010) 'Mutual augmentation of surveillance practices on social media', PhD thesis, Queen's University.

Urry, J. (2000) *Sociology beyond Societies: Mobilities for the Twenty-First Century*. London: Routledge.

Urry, J. (2002) *The Tourist Gaze*. 2nd edn, London: Sage.

Van Dijck, J. (2005) 'Mediated memories: personal cultural memory as objects of cultural analysis', *Continuum*, 18(2): 261–77.

Van Dijck, J. (2007) *Mediated Memories in the Digital Age*. Stanford, CA: Stanford University Press.

Van Dijck, J. (2008) 'Digital photography: communication, identity, memory', *Visual Communication*, 7(1): 57–76.

Van Dijck, J. (2011) 'Flickr and the culture of connectivity: sharing views, experiences, memories', *Memory Studies*, 4(4): 401–15.

Van House, N. A. (2007) 'Flickr and public image-sharing: distant closeness and photo exhibition', *Extended Abstracts on Human Factors in Computing Systems*; available at: http://people.ischool.berkeley.edu/~vanhouse/VanHouseFlickrDistantCHI07.pdf.

Van House, N. A. (2009) 'Collocated photo sharing, story-telling, and the performance of self', *International Journal of Human–Computer Interaction*, 67: 1073–86.

Van House, N. A. (2011) 'Personal photography, digital technologies, and the uses of the visual', *Visual Studies*, 25(1): 125–34.

Van House, N., and Churchill, E. (2008) 'Technologies of memory: key issues and critical perspectives', *Memory Studies*, 1(3): 295–310.

Van House, N. A., Davis, M., Takhteyev, Y., Good, N., Wilhelm, A., and Finn, M. (2004) 'From "what?" to "why?": the social uses of personal photos', available at: http://people.ischool.berkeley.edu/~vanhouse/van%20house_et_al_2004a.pdf.

Van House, N. A., Davis, M., Ames, M., Finn, M., and Viswanathan, V. (2005) 'The uses of personal networked digital imaging: an empirical study of cameraphone photos and sharing', *Extended Abstracts on Human Factors in Computing Systems*; available at: http://citeseer.ist.psu.edu/viewdoc/summary?doi=10.1.1.114.6563.

Vattimo, G. (1990) *The Transparent Society*. Cambridge: Polity.

Veblen, T. ([1899] 1953) *Theory of the Leisure Class*. New York: Mentor.

Warde, A. (2005) 'Consumption and theories of practice', *Journal of Consumer Culture*, 5(2): 131–53.

Warde, A. (2010) 'Consumption and critique', in J. Hall, L. Grindstaff and L. Ming-Cheng, eds, *Handbook of Cultural Sociology*. London: Routledge.

Wellman, B., and Haythornthwaite, C., eds (2002) *The Internet in Everyday Life*. Oxford: Blackwell.

Wells, L., ed. (2009) *Photography: A Critical Introduction*. 4th edn, London: Routledge.

West, N. M. (2000) *Kodak and the Lens of Nostalgia*. Charlottesville: University of Virginia Press.

Williams, R. (1974) *Television, Technology and Cultural Form*. London: Fontana.

Winston, B. (1995) *Claiming the Real*. London: British Film Institute.

Woolgar, S. (2002) *Virtual Society? Technology, Cyberbole, Reality*. Oxford: Oxford University Press.

Zuckerman, M. E. (1998) *A History of Popular Women's Magazines in the United States, 1792–1995*. Westport, CT: Greenwood Press.

Websites

InfoTrends: the leading worldwide market research and strategic consulting firm for the digital imaging and document solutions industry: www.infotrends.com/public/home.html.
Digital Photography Review: www.dpreview.com/.

BBC News, 'Your news, your pictures': http://news.bbc.co.uk/2/hi/talking_point/2780295.stm.

The Dead Photographers Project: an expanding collection of images which explore the relationship of photography and our changing times: www.deadphotographers.co.uk.

CBC NewsCommunity's photo stream: www.flickr.com/photos/cbcy-ourvoice/.

Craft-orientated websites offering online photo storage, printing, sharing, enhancing and messaging: www.shutterfly.com/; www.snapfish.com/.

Repository of professional and amateur images: www.webshots.com/.

Photographic Historical Society of Canada: http://phsc.ca/.

Index